BEYOND THE ALGORITHM: THE RISE OF GENERATIVE AI AND LLM

DR.D.VENKATA LAKSHMI

DR.C.KOTTEESWARAN

DR.G.A.SENTHIL

DR.S.GEERTHIK

Contents

CHAPTER ONE

INTRODUCTION

In the annals of technological advancement, few epochs have been as transformative as the current era of artificial intelligence (AI). At the forefront of this revolution stand generative AI and Large Language Models (LLMs), technologies that are reshaping industries, challenging traditional boundaries, and redefining the very nature of human creativity and interaction. This book embarks on a journey to explore the genesis, evolution, and profound implications of these groundbreaking innovations.

Generative AI, with its ability to generate new content, has unleashed a wave of creativity and innovation across diverse domains. From crafting stunning visuals and composing captivating music to writing compelling narratives and designing functional products, generative AI is demonstrating its potential to augment human capabilities and drive unprecedented levels of productivity. LLMs, on the other hand, have revolutionized natural language processing by enabling machines to understand, interpret, and generate human language in ways that were once unimaginable. Their applications span from customer service and content creation to education and research, promising to transform the way we communicate and interact with information.

As we delve into the intricacies of generative AI and LLMs, we will examine their underlying principles, explore their diverse applications, and grapple with the ethical considerations that accompany their rapid development. From the early pioneers who laid the groundwork to the cutting-edge research that continues to push the boundaries, this book will provide a comprehensive overview of the journey that has brought us to the brink of a new AI revolution.

In the annals of technological advancement, few epochs have been as transformative as the current era of artificial intelligence. At the forefront of this revolution stands a new breed of AI models: generative AI and large language models (LLMs). These sophisticated systems, capable of learning from vast datasets and generating human-quality content, are poised to redefine industries, alter our daily lives, and reshape the very fabric of society.

CHAPTER TWO

THE FOUNDATIONS OF ARTIFICIAL INTELLIGENCE

Artificial intelligence (AI), once a realm of science fiction, has become an integral part of our modern world. Its roots lie in the ambitious pursuit of creating machines that can think, learn, and reason like humans. The foundation of AI is built upon a complex interplay of theoretical concepts, mathematical models, and technological advancements. From the early days of neural networks to the sophisticated algorithms of today, AI has evolved rapidly, laying the groundwork for a future where intelligent machines augment human capabilities and revolutionize various industries. The tapestry of artificial intelligence (AI) is woven with threads of intricate concepts, mathematical models, and technological innovations. It is a field that has emerged from the intersection of computer science, mathematics, and cognitive science, aspiring to create intelligent machines that can mimic human thought processes and capabilities. The foundations of AI are laid upon a bedrock of theoretical frameworks, such as neural networks and machine learning algorithms, that enable machines to learn from data, recognize patterns, and make informed decisions. From the early days of rule-based systems to the sophisticated deep learning architectures of today, the evolution of AI has been marked by significant advancements, paving the way for a future where intelligent machines seamlessly integrate into our lives, transforming industries and reshaping society. Artificial intelligence (AI), once a realm of science fiction, has become an integral part of our modern world. Its roots lie in the ambitious pursuit of creating machines that can think, learn, and reason like humans. The foundation of AI is built upon a complex interplay of theoretical concepts, mathematical models, and technological advancements. From the early days of neural networks to the sophisticated algorithms of today, AI has evolved rapidly, laying the groundwork for a future where intelligent machines augment human capabilities and revolutionize various industries. The tapestry of artificial intelligence (AI) is woven with threads of diverse disciplines, each contributing to its intricate and evolving nature. At its core, AI rests upon a foundation of mathematical models, computational techniques, and philosophical inquiries. These foundational elements, intertwined and mutually reinforcing, have shaped the trajectory of AI research and development, paving the way for the remarkable advancements we witness today. From the early pioneers' dreams of creating intelligent machines to the sophisticated algorithms that power our world, the foundations of AI continue to be the bedrock upon which the future of technology is being built.

THE GENESIS OF AI: A HISTORICAL OVERVIEW

The concept of artificial intelligence (AI) has been a tantalizing dream for centuries, dating back to ancient myths and philosophical musings. However, it wasn't until the mid-20th century that AI began to take concrete form. Pioneers like Alan Turing, the father of computer science, laid the theoretical groundwork for AI with his vision of machines capable of intelligent behaviour. Early AI research focused on developing problem-solving algorithms and rule-based systems, but limitations in computing power and data availability hindered significant progress.

The resurgence of AI in the 1980s and 1990s was fuelled by advancements in hardware and the development of neural networks, a type of machine learning model inspired by the human brain. Neural networks offered a more flexible and adaptive approach to AI, enabling machines to learn from data and improve their performance over time. The AI winter of the 1990s, characterized by a decline in funding and interest, was followed by a renewed surge in AI research and development in the 21st century, driven by the availability of massive datasets and breakthroughs in deep learning techniques.

1. Early Visions and Philosophical Musings

The concept of artificial intelligence (AI) has deep roots in human history, dating back to ancient civilizations. While the term "artificial intelligence" itself didn't exist until the 20th century, the idea of creating intelligent machines has been a recurring theme in human imagination for millennia.

Ancient Greek Philosophy:

One of the earliest recorded explorations of AI-like concepts can be found in the works of ancient Greek philosophers. Aristotle, for example, envisioned a self-moving automaton, a mechanical device capable of performing tasks without human intervention. This idea laid the groundwork for the development of automata and mechanical devices in later centuries.

Medieval Automata and Mechanical Figures:

During the Middle Ages, there was a resurgence of interest in creating mechanical figures and automata. Scholars and artisans experimented with complex mechanisms that could perform various tasks, such as playing musical instruments or moving limbs. These early automata were often seen as marvels of engineering and were often associated with magic or the supernatural.

Philosophical Speculations:

Beyond the practical applications of automata, philosophers and thinkers throughout history have pondered the possibility of creating artificial beings with intelligence. René Descartes, a 17th-century French philosopher, speculated about the creation of mechanical animals that could mimic human behavior. Later, philosophers like Gottfried Wilhelm Leibniz and Blaise Pascal explored the potential for machines to reason and think logically.

The Limitations of Early Conceptions:

While these early visions and philosophical musings laid the foundation for the development of AI, they were limited by the technological constraints of their time. The lack of advanced materials, computational power, and understanding of the human mind prevented the realization of truly intelligent machines. It wasn't until the 20th century that the necessary tools and knowledge became available to begin the serious pursuit of AI.

2. The Birth of Computer Science and AI

The foundation for modern AI was laid by Alan Turing, a British mathematician and computer scientist. In his 1950 paper "Computing Machinery and Intelligence," Turing proposed the Turing Test, a method to determine if a machine could exhibit intelligent behaviour indistinguishable from a human. Turing's work, along with the development of early computers, paved the way for the emergence of AI as a distinct field of study.

The Turing Test: A Benchmark for Intelligence

In his 1950 paper "Computing Machinery and Intelligence," Turing proposed a thought experiment known as the Turing Test. The test involves a human judge who communicates with a human and a machine through a text-only interface. If the judge cannot reliably distinguish between the human and the machine, then the machine can be considered intelligent. The Turing Test has become a widely accepted benchmark for evaluating the intelligence of AI systems.

The Enigma Machine and the War Effort

During World War II, Turing made significant contributions to the British war effort by cracking the Enigma code, a German encryption machine used to communicate with submarines. His work on codebreaking helped to shorten the war and is considered one of the greatest intellectual achievements of the 20th century.

Pioneering Work in Computer Science

Alan Turing's contributions to computer science extended far beyond his groundbreaking work on codebreaking during World

War II. One of his most significant achievements was the development of the universal Turing machine, a theoretical model of a computer that can compute any computable function. This concept laid the foundation for modern computer architecture and programming languages. The universal Turing machine is a simple but powerful model that consists of a finite-state machine with an infinite tape. The machine can read and write symbols on the tape, move left or right, and change its state based on the current symbol and its internal state. Turing showed that this simple model can simulate any other Turing machine, making it a universal computing device. The concept of the universal Turing machine has had a profound impact on computer science. It has helped researchers understand the fundamental limits of computation and has been used as a theoretical tool for analyzing the complexity of algorithms. Furthermore, the universal Turing machine has served as a blueprint for the design of real-world computers, inspiring the development of modern computer architectures and programming languages.

Turing's work on the universal Turing machine not only laid the foundation for modern computer science but also helped to establish the theoretical basis for artificial intelligence. Turing's vision of a machine that could think and reason has inspired generations of researchers and continues to drive the development of AI today.

3. The Legacy of Turing

Turing's visionary work had a profound impact on the development of AI. His ideas about intelligence, computation, and the potential of machines to think and reason laid the groundwork for the field of AI research. Turing's legacy continues to inspire scientists and researchers around the world, as they strive to create intelligent machines that can surpass human capabilities. Alan Turing's contributions to computer science and AI have had a profound and lasting impact on the field. His visionary work has inspired generations of researchers and has laid the foundation for many of the advancements in AI that we see today.

The Turing Test: A Benchmark for Intelligence

One of Turing's most significant contributions was the development of the Turing Test. This thought experiment, proposed in his 1950 paper "Computing Machinery and Intelligence," has become a widely accepted benchmark for evaluating the intelligence of AI systems. By challenging humans to distinguish between a human and a machine through text-only communication, the Turing Test provides a measure of a machine's ability to exhibit human-like intelligence.

The Universal Turing Machine: A Theoretical Foundation

Turing's concept of the universal Turing machine, a theoretical model of a computer that can compute any computable function, has been fundamental to the development of modern computer architecture and programming languages. The universal Turing machine demonstrated the theoretical limits of computation and provided a framework for understanding the capabilities and limitations of computers.

The Father of Computer Science

Turing is often referred to as the "father of computer science" due to his pioneering work in the field. His contributions to theoretical computer science, including his work on computability theory and the foundations of algorithms, have had a profound impact on the development of modern computing technology.

Inspiration for Future Generations

Turing's legacy continues to inspire researchers and scientists around the world. His work has shown the potential for machines to exhibit intelligence and has encouraged the pursuit of AI research. Turing's vision of a future where machines can think and reason like humans remains a driving force for many in the field of AI. Alan Turing's contributions to computer science and AI have been invaluable. His work on the Turing Test, the universal Turing machine, and the foundations of computer science has laid the groundwork for many of the advancements in AI that we see today. Turing's legacy will continue to inspire future generations of researchers as they strive to push the boundaries of what is possible in the field of artificial intelligence.

4. The Early Years of AI Research

The 1950s and 1960s marked a period of intense excitement and exploration in the field of artificial intelligence (AI). Scientists and researchers, inspired by the groundbreaking work of Alan Turing and others, began to delve into the possibilities of creating intelligent machines.

Rule-Based Systems: Early AI Pioneers

One of the earliest approaches to AI was the development of rule-based systems. These systems relied on a set of predefined rules and facts to make decisions and solve problems. Early examples of rule-based systems included expert systems, which were designed to mimic the reasoning of human experts in specific domains.

The Rise of Neural Networks: A New Paradigm

Another significant development during this period was the emergence of neural networks. Inspired by the structure and function of the human brain, neural networks are computational models that can learn from data and improve their performance over time. Early neural networks were relatively simple, but they demonstrated the potential for AI systems to adapt and learn from experience.

Problem-Solving Algorithms: A Focus on Logic and Reasoning

In addition to rule-based systems and neural networks, researchers also explored problem-solving algorithms. These algorithms were designed to solve specific types of problems, such as mathematical equations or puzzles. Early AI programs achieved notable successes in domains like theorem proving and game playing, demonstrating the power of logic and reasoning in AI.

Early AI Successes: Chess, Theorem Proving, and Natural Language Processing

The early years of AI research saw several significant breakthroughs. AI programs were developed that could defeat human chess champions, prove complex mathematical theorems, and understand and generate human language. These successes helped to solidify AI as a viable field of study and generated excitement about the potential for AI to revolutionize various industries.

The 1950s and 1960s were a time of great innovation and experimentation in the field of AI. Researchers explored various approaches to creating intelligent machines, laying the foundation for the advancements that would follow in the decades to come. While the early years of AI research were marked by both successes and challenges, the pioneering work of these early researchers paved the way for the development of the sophisticated AI systems we see today.

6. The AI Winter and Setbacks

Despite the initial optimism, the 1970s and 1980s witnessed a period of disillusionment known as the "AI winter." Expectations for AI progress were not met, and funding for AI research declined. Factors contributing to the AI winter included limitations in computing power, the complexity of real-world problems, and the challenges of developing truly intelligent systems.

Limitations in Computing Power:

One of the primary constraints during this period was the limited computing power available. Early AI systems were heavily reliant on large, expensive computers, which were often slow and inefficient. The lack of sufficient computational resources hindered the development of more complex AI models and applications.

The Complexity of Real-World Problems:

AI researchers soon realized that real-world problems were far more complex than the simplified tasks they had initially focused on. Issues such as ambiguity, uncertainty, and noise in data made it difficult for AI systems to perform reliably in real-world scenarios.

Challenges in Developing Truly Intelligent Systems:

The early AI systems often lacked the ability to exhibit true intelligence. They were often limited to specific tasks and were unable to generalize their knowledge to new situations. The challenges of developing AI systems that could reason, learn, and adapt like humans were significant.

The Impact of the AI Winter

The AI winter had a profound impact on the field of AI research. Funding for AI projects declined, and many researchers left the field. The overall momentum and excitement surrounding AI development waned, and the field entered a period of stagnation.

The AI winter was a difficult time for the AI community. However, the challenges faced during this period also led to important lessons and advancements. Researchers learned from their mistakes and developed new approaches to AI research. The AI winter ultimately paved the way for the resurgence of AI in the late 20th and early 21st centuries.

7. The Resurgence of AI:

The late 20th and early 21st centuries marked a resurgence of AI research and development. Advancements in hardware, the availability of large datasets, and breakthroughs in machine learning techniques, particularly deep learning, fuelled a new era of AI. Deep learning models, inspired by the structure of the human brain, have enabled AI systems to achieve remarkable performance in tasks such as image recognition, natural language processing, and game playing.

Advancements in Hardware:

One of the key drivers of the AI renaissance was the rapid advancement of hardware technology. Moore's Law, which predicted the doubling of computing power every two years, continued to hold true, providing AI researchers with increasingly powerful machines to work with. This increased computational capacity enabled the development of more complex AI models and the processing of larger datasets.

The Explosion of Data:

The digital age has led to an exponential growth in the amount of data generated. This data deluge, spanning various domains such as social media, e-commerce, and scientific research, has provided AI researchers with a rich source of information to train and improve their models. The availability of large datasets has been instrumental in driving breakthroughs in machine learning and AI applications.

Breakthroughs in Machine Learning:

Perhaps the most significant development during this period has been the breakthroughs in machine learning techniques, particularly deep learning. Deep learning models, inspired by the structure of the human brain, are capable of learning complex patterns and representations from large amounts of data. This has enabled AI systems to achieve remarkable performance in tasks such as image recognition, natural language processing, and game playing.

Transformative Applications of AI:

The resurgence of AI has led to a wide range of transformative applications across various industries. AI is being used to improve healthcare outcomes, enhance customer experiences, optimize business processes, and even develop self-driving cars. The potential of AI to revolutionize society is immense, and we are only beginning to scratch the surface of its capabilities.

The resurgence of AI in recent decades has been driven by advancements in hardware, the availability of large datasets, and breakthroughs in machine learning techniques. This new era of AI is characterized by the development of powerful and versatile AI systems that are capable of solving complex problems and transforming industries. As AI continues to evolve, we can expect to see even more remarkable achievements and applications in the years to come.

EARLY PIONEERS AND CONCEPTS

The Ancient Roots of AI

The concept of artificial intelligence (AI) has deep historical roots, tracing back to ancient myths and philosophical musings. Ancient civilizations envisioned intelligent machines and automata, often imbued with supernatural powers or magical abilities. These early conceptions laid the groundwork for the development of AI as a field of study.

The Modern Era of AI Research

The modern era of AI research began in the mid-20th century, inspired by the groundbreaking work of early pioneers. Alan Turing, John McCarthy, and Marvin Minsky were among the most influential figures in shaping the course of AI development.

Alan Turing: The Turing Test

Alan Turing, a British mathematician and computer scientist, proposed the Turing Test in his 1950 paper "Computing Machinery and Intelligence." This test serves as a benchmark for determining whether a machine can exhibit intelligent behavior indistinguishable from a human. If a machine can convince a human evaluator that it is a human, it is said to have passed the Turing Test.

John McCarthy: The Father of AI

John McCarthy, a pioneer in AI research, coined the term "artificial intelligence" and organized the Dartmouth Conference in 1956, which is often considered the birth of AI as a field of study. The Dartmouth Conference brought together a group of leading researchers to discuss the potential of AI and explore its applications.

Marvin Minsky: A Visionary in AI

Marvin Minsky, another key figure in the early days of AI, was a co-founder of the Massachusetts Institute of Technology's Artificial Intelligence Laboratory (MIT AI Lab). He made significant contributions to the development of AI techniques and applications, including work on neural networks, robotics, and natural language processing.

Together, Turing, McCarthy, and Minsky, along with other early AI pioneers, laid the foundation for the field of AI and paved the way for future advancements. Their work continues to inspire and guide researchers as they explore the potential of AI to transform society.

The Benchmark for Intelligent Machines

The Turing Test, proposed by Alan Turing, has become a widely recognized benchmark for evaluating the intelligence of AI systems. It involves a human judge who communicates with a human and a machine through a text-only interface. If the judge cannot reliably distinguish between the human and the machine, then the machine can be considered intelligent. The Turing Test has been used to assess the capabilities of AI systems in areas such as natural language processing, problem-solving, and creativity.

The AI Winter: Challenges and Setbacks

Despite the initial optimism and early successes, the 1970s and 1980s witnessed a period of disillusionment known as the "AI winter." Expectations for AI progress were not met, and funding for AI research declined. Several factors contributed to this downturn:

- **Limitations in computing power:** Early AI systems were heavily reliant on large, expensive computers, which were often slow and inefficient. The lack of sufficient computational resources hindered the development of more complex AI models and applications.
- **The complexity of real-world problems:** AI researchers soon realized that real-world problems were far more complex than the simplified tasks they had initially focused on. Issues such as ambiguity, uncertainty, and noise in data made it difficult for AI systems to perform reliably in real-world scenarios.
- **Challenges in developing truly intelligent systems:** The early AI systems often lacked the ability to exhibit true intelligence. They were often limited to specific tasks and were unable to generalize their knowledge to new situations. The challenges of developing AI systems that could reason, learn, and adapt like humans were significant.

The AI winter had a profound impact on the field of AI research. Funding for AI projects declined, and many researchers left the field. The overall momentum and excitement surrounding AI development waned, and the field entered a period of stagnation.

THE RESURGENCE OF AI

The resurgence of AI in the late 20th and early 21st centuries was fueled in part by the development of neural networks. Inspired by the structure and function of the human brain, neural networks are computational models that can learn from data and improve their performance over time.

Early Neural Networks: Early neural networks were relatively simple, consisting of a few layers of interconnected nodes. These early models demonstrated the potential of AI systems to learn from data and adapt to new situations.

The Backpropagation Algorithm: A breakthrough in neural network training came with the development of the backpropagation algorithm. This algorithm allows neural networks to learn from their mistakes and gradually improve their performance.

Deep Learning: The advent of deep learning, which involves training neural networks with multiple layers, has led to a revolution in AI. Deep learning models have achieved remarkable performance in tasks such as image recognition, natural language processing, and game playing.

The Data Revolution: Fuelling AI's Advancements

The availability of massive datasets has been another key factor in the resurgence of AI. The digital age has led to an explosion of data, from social media posts and e-commerce transactions to scientific experiments and satellite imagery. This abundance of data provides AI researchers with a rich source of information to train and improve their models.

The term "big data" refers to datasets that are so large or complex that traditional data processing techniques are inadequate. The ability to process and analyse big data has been essential for the development of advanced AI systems. AI research has increasingly shifted towards data-driven approaches, where models are trained on large datasets to learn patterns and relationships that would be difficult for humans to identify.

The Age of Deep Learning: Breakthroughs and Applications

Deep learning has emerged as a dominant paradigm in AI research. Deep neural networks, with their ability to learn complex representations from data, have led to breakthroughs in a wide range of applications.

Computer Vision: Deep learning has revolutionized computer vision, enabling machines to recognize objects, detect faces, and understand visual scenes with unprecedented accuracy.

Natural Language Processing: AI systems powered by deep learning can now understand and generate human language, leading to advancements in machine translation, text summarization, and chatbots.

Speech Recognition: Deep learning has significantly improved the accuracy of speech recognition systems, enabling voice-controlled devices and virtual assistants to become more accessible and reliable.

Generative Models: Deep learning models can also be used to generate new content, such as images, music, and text. This has led to the development of creative AI applications, such as style transfer and image generation.

The resurgence of AI, fuelled by advancements in neural networks, the availability of large datasets, and the power of deep learning, has ushered in a new era of innovation and opportunity. As AI continues to evolve, we can expect to see even more remarkable breakthroughs and applications in the years to come.

CHAPTER THREE

THE BUILDING BLOCKS OF NEURAL NETWORKS AND DEEP LEARNING

In recent years, the field of artificial intelligence has witnessed a groundbreaking revolution with the emergence of generative AI and large language models (LLMs). These powerful technologies are reshaping industries, challenging traditional boundaries, and ushering in a new era of innovation. From creating stunning artwork to answering complex questions, generative AI and LLMs are demonstrating their immense potential to transform our lives in unprecedented ways. This exploration delves into the fundamental concepts, evolution, applications, and ethical considerations surrounding these transformative technologies, providing a comprehensive understanding of the building blocks that are shaping the future of AI. Neural networks and deep learning have revolutionized the field of artificial intelligence, enabling machines to learn complex patterns and make intelligent decisions. Inspired by the structure and function of the human brain, these powerful tools are composed of interconnected layers of artificial neurons that process information. By understanding the fundamental building blocks of neural networks and deep learning, we can gain insights into how these systems learn, evolve, and shape our world. This exploration delves into the core concepts, components, and applications of neural networks and deep learning, providing a solid foundation for understanding the driving forces behind artificial intelligence's remarkable advancements.

NEURAL NETWORKS

Neural networks are computational models inspired by the structure and function of the human brain. They are composed of interconnected nodes, or neurons, that process information in a similar way to biological neurons. These networks are capable of learning complex patterns from data, making them powerful tools for a wide range of applications.

The Role of Neurons

Neurons are the fundamental units of neural networks, analogous to the biological neurons in the human brain. Each neuron receives input signals, processes them, and generates an output signal. This process is essential for neural networks to learn and make decisions.

Input Signals:

- Dendrites: Neurons receive input signals through their dendrites. These are branching extensions that connect to other neurons or external sources.
- Synapses: The connections between neurons are called synapses. When a neuron fires, it sends electrical signals through its axon, which can trigger the firing of connected neurons.

Processing Input Signals:

- Weighted Sum: The input signals are weighted to reflect their relative importance. This weighting is essential for the network to learn patterns and relationships in the data.
- Activation Function: The weighted sum of the input signals is then passed through an activation function. This function introduces nonlinearity into the network, enabling it to learn complex patterns that cannot be captured by linear models.

Output Signal:

- Axon: The output of a neuron is generated and transmitted through its axon. This signal can then be used as input for other neurons in the network.

In essence, neurons act as computational units that process information and transmit it to other neurons, forming the interconnected structure of a neural network.

Activation Functions:

Activation functions are essential components of neural networks that introduce nonlinearity into the network's computations. This nonlinearity is crucial for learning complex patterns and relationships in data. Without activation functions, neural networks would be limited to linear models, which are unable to capture the intricacies of many real-world problems.

Common Activation Functions:

ReLU (Rectified Linear Unit):

Formula: $ReLU(x) = max(0, x)$

Explanation: ReLU returns the input if it's positive, or 0 otherwise. This simple function has several advantages:

- Computational Efficiency: ReLU is computationally efficient compared to other activation functions, as it involves a simple threshold operation.
- Avoiding the Vanishing Gradient Problem: ReLU helps to mitigate the vanishing gradient problem, which can occur in deep neural networks when gradients become very small during training, making it difficult for the network to learn.

Sigmoid:

Formula: $Sigmoid(x) = 1 / (1 + exp(-x))$

Explanation: Sigmoid returns a value between 0 and 1, making it suitable for tasks like binary classification where the output is a probability. It was commonly used in the past, but has been largely replaced by ReLU due to its computational efficiency and the vanishing gradient problem.

Tanh:

Formula: Tanh(x) = (exp(x) - exp(-x)) / (exp(x) + exp(-x))

Explanation: Tanh is similar to sigmoid but returns values between -1 and 1. It is often used in recurrent neural networks (RNNs) due to its zero-centered output.

The Role of Activation Functions:

- **Introducing Nonlinearity:** Activation functions introduce nonlinearity into the network, allowing it to learn complex patterns that cannot be captured by linear models.
- **Determining Neuron Output:** The activation function determines the output of a neuron based on the weighted sum of its inputs.
- **Impact on Network Behaviour:** The choice of activation function can significantly impact the behaviour and performance of a neural network.

In summary, activation functions play a vital role in shaping the behaviour and learning capabilities of neural networks. By understanding the properties and characteristics of different activation functions, you can make informed choices when designing and training neural network models.

BUILDING NEURAL NETWORKS

The Structure of Neural Networks

Neural networks are typically organized into layers, each containing multiple interconnected neurons. These layers work together to process and analyze data. The three primary types of layers are:

1. Input Layer:

- Purpose: Receives the raw input data.
- Structure: The number of neurons in the input layer corresponds to the dimensionality of the input data. For

example, if the input is an image with 28x28 pixels, the input layer would have 784 neurons.

2. Hidden Layers:

* Purpose: Process and transform the input data to extract relevant features.
* Structure: The number of hidden layers and neurons within each layer determines the network's complexity and learning capacity. Deeper networks with more hidden layers can learn more complex patterns and relationships.

3. Output Layer:

* Purpose: Produces the final output or prediction.
* Structure: The number of neurons in the output layer depends on the task. For example, in a binary classification problem, the output layer might have one neuron with a sigmoid activation function to produce a probability between 0 and 1.

The complexity of a neural network is largely determined by the number of layers and neurons. Deeper networks with more layers can learn more complex patterns, but they also require more computational resources to train. Additionally, the choice of activation functions for each neuron can influence the network's behavior and learning capabilities.

In summary, the layered structure of neural networks allows them to process and analyze data in a hierarchical manner, enabling them to learn complex patterns and make accurate predictions.

Connections and Weights:

Connections between neurons form the intricate web that defines the structure of a neural network. These connections are akin to synapses in the human brain, where electrical signals are transmitted between neurons. Each connection has an associated weight that determines the strength of the signal passing through it.

- Positive Weights: Stronger positive weights indicate a stronger excitatory connection, meaning the neuron is more likely to activate the connected neuron.
- Negative Weights: Negative weights represent inhibitory connections, making the connected neuron less likely to activate.

The weights in a neural network are crucial for its learning process. Initially, these weights are typically initialized randomly. During training, the network learns to adjust these weights based on the input data and the desired output.

Backpropagation:

Backpropagation is a key algorithm used to train neural networks. It involves calculating the error between the network's predicted output and the actual target output. This error is then propagated backward through the network, allowing the weights to be adjusted in a way that reduces the error.

- **Gradient Descent:** Backpropagation often uses gradient descent to update the weights. This involves calculating the gradient of the error function with respect to the weights and adjusting them in the direction that minimizes the error.
- **Weight Updates:** The weights are updated iteratively based on the calculated gradients. This process continues until the network converges to a satisfactory solution.

In essence, the connections and weights in a neural network define its structure and learning capacity. By adjusting the weights through backpropagation, the network can learn complex patterns and relationships in the data.

Training Neural Networks:

Training a neural network involves repeatedly exposing it to large amounts of data and adjusting its weights to minimize the difference between its predicted outputs and the desired correct outputs. This process is akin to teaching a child by showing them

many examples and providing feedback.
Iterative Training:

- Data is often divided into batches to improve computational efficiency.
- A complete pass through the entire dataset is called an epoch. Multiple epochs are typically required for effective training.
- Training continues until the network's performance stops improving significantly or reaches a predefined threshold.

Optimization Algorithms:

- This algorithm calculates the gradient of the error function with respect to the weights and adjusts them in the direction that minimizes the error. It's a popular but computationally expensive method.
- Stochastic Gradient Descent (SGD): SGD updates the weights based on a single training example at a time, making it faster and more suitable for large datasets.
- Adam: A more recent algorithm that combines the best aspects of several other algorithms, including adaptive learning rates and momentum. It's often the preferred choice for training deep neural networks.

Key Considerations:

- Hyperparameters: The choice of hyperparameters, such as learning rate, batch size, and the number of hidden layers, can significantly impact the network's performance.
- Overfitting: Networks can become overfitted if they learn the training data too well, leading to poor generalization to new data. Techniques like regularization can help prevent overfitting.
- Underfitting: Networks can also underfit if they are not complex enough to capture the underlying patterns in the data. Increasing the network's complexity or providing more data can

help address underfitting.

The training process and the various optimization algorithms available, you can effectively train neural networks to solve a wide range of tasks.

DEEP LEARNING

Deep learning, a subset of machine learning, has emerged as a transformative technology with the potential to revolutionize various industries. At its core, deep learning involves training artificial neural networks with multiple hidden layers to recognize complex patterns and features within data. These deeper networks enable machines to learn from vast amounts of data, extracting higher-level representations that are crucial for tasks like image recognition, natural language processing, and speech recognition. Unlike traditional machine learning algorithms, deep learning models can automatically learn relevant features from raw data, eliminating the need for manual feature engineering. This capability has led to significant advancements in fields such as computer vision, natural language processing, and healthcare, where deep learning models have achieved remarkable results that were previously unattainable.

Convolutional Neural Networks (CNNs) for Image Processing

Convolutional Neural Networks (CNNs) are a specialized type of neural network designed for processing image data. They are composed of convolutional layers, pooling layers, and fully connected layers.

- **Convolutional Layers:** These layers apply filters to the input image, extracting features such as edges, corners, and textures.
- **Pooling Layers:** These layers down sample the feature maps, reducing the dimensionality of the data while preserving important information.
- **Fully Connected Layers:** The final layers in a CNN are typically fully connected layers, similar to those used in traditional neural networks.

CNNs have been extremely successful in tasks such as image classification, object detection, and image generation.

Recurrent Neural Networks (RNNs) for Sequential Data

Recurrent Neural Networks (RNNs) are designed to process sequential data, such as text, time series, and audio. Unlike traditional feedforward neural networks, RNNs have feedback connections that allow them to maintain information about previous inputs. This makes them well-suited for tasks that require understanding context and dependencies.

- Simple RNNs: The simplest type of RNN, but they can struggle to remember information from long sequences.
- Long Short-Term Memory (LSTM) Networks: A more powerful type of RNN that uses gates to control the flow of information, allowing them to learn long-term dependencies.
- Gated Recurrent Units (GRUs): A simplified version of LSTM networks that are computationally more efficient.

RNNs have been used for tasks such as machine translation, speech recognition, and text generation.

APPLICATIONS AND IMPACT

Neural networks and deep learning have revolutionized various industries, enabling breakthroughs in a wide range of applications. Here are some notable examples:

Deep Learning Applications: A Comprehensive Overview

Deep learning has revolutionized various fields by enabling machines to learn complex patterns and features from data. Here are some of the most prominent applications of deep learning:

Image Recognition and Computer Vision

Image Classification: Deep learning models can accurately classify images into different categories, such as identifying objects, animals, or scenes. For instance, a deep learning model can distinguish between cats and dogs in images.

Object Detection: Deep learning algorithms can locate and recognize objects within images, drawing bounding boxes around them and labeling them accurately. This is crucial for applications like autonomous vehicles and surveillance systems.

Facial Recognition: Deep learning models can be trained to recognize individual faces, enabling applications like access control, law enforcement, and social media tagging.

Medical Image Analysis: Deep learning has made significant strides in medical image analysis, assisting in tasks like diagnosing diseases from X-rays, MRIs, and CT scans. For example, deep learning models can detect tumors or abnormalities in medical images.

Natural Language Processing (NLP)

Machine Translation: Deep learning-based machine translation systems can translate text from one language to another with high accuracy, facilitating global communication.

Text Summarization: Deep learning models can summarize long texts into shorter, more concise summaries, making it easier to digest information.

Sentiment Analysis: These models can analyze text to determine the sentiment expressed (positive, negative, or neutral), enabling applications like social media monitoring and market research.

Chatbots and Virtual Assistants: Deep learning-powered chatbots and virtual assistants can engage in natural language conversations, providing information, completing tasks, and offering personalized recommendations.

Speech Recognition and Synthesis

Voice Assistants: Deep learning has enabled the development of highly accurate voice assistants like Siri, Alexa, and Google Assistant, which can understand and respond to spoken commands.

Speech-to-Text Transcription: Deep learning models can transcribe spoken language into text, enabling applications like transcription services, captioning, and voice-controlled devices.

Text-to-Speech Synthesis: Deep learning can generate realistic-sounding speech from text, enabling applications like audiobooks, language learning, and accessibility tools for visually impaired individuals.

Drug Discovery and Development

Identifying Potential Drug Candidates: Deep learning models can analyze vast amounts of chemical and biological data to identify potential drug candidates.

Predicting Drug-Target Interactions: Deep learning can predict how drugs interact with target proteins, helping to accelerate the drug discovery process.

Autonomous Vehicles

Perception: Deep learning is crucial for autonomous vehicles to perceive their surroundings, including detecting objects, pedestrians, and traffic signs.

Decision-Making: Deep learning models can help autonomous vehicles make decisions, such as planning routes, avoiding obstacles, and responding to unexpected situations.

Recommendation Systems

Suggesting Products or Content: Deep learning-powered recommendation systems can analyze user data to suggest products, movies, music, or other content that aligns with their preferences. This is widely used in e-commerce, streaming services, and social media platforms.

The Future of AI:

The field of AI, driven by advancements in neural networks and deep learning, is rapidly evolving. Some emerging trends and possibilities include:

- Developing AI models that can provide transparent explanations for their decisions, enhancing trust and accountability.
- Leveraging AI to address societal challenges, such as healthcare, education, and climate change.
- Establishing ethical guidelines and regulations to ensure responsible and beneficial AI development.
- Exploring ways for AI to augment human capabilities and create new opportunities.
- Integrating AI into everyday devices and services, making them more intelligent and personalized.

CHAPTER FOUR

THE DATA REVOLUTION

The advent of the digital age has ushered in a data revolution, characterized by the exponential growth and accessibility of information. This data deluge has become the lifeblood of artificial intelligence (AI), fueling its rapid advancements and transforming industries across the globe. From personalized recommendations to autonomous vehicles, AI's remarkable achievements are inextricably linked to the availability and quality of data. This exploration delves into the pivotal role of data in driving AI's progress, examining the challenges and opportunities presented by the data revolution, and envisioning the future of AI in a data-centric world. The digital age has ushered in a data revolution, characterized by the exponential growth and accessibility of information. This data deluge has become the lifeblood of artificial intelligence (AI), fueling its rapid advancements and transforming industries across the globe. From personalized recommendations to autonomous vehicles, AI's remarkable achievements are inextricably linked to the availability and quality of data. This exploration delves into the pivotal role of data in driving AI's progress, examining the challenges and opportunities presented by the data revolution, and envisioning the future of AI in a data-centric world. Data serves as the foundation upon which AI models are built. It provides the raw material that AI systems learn from, allowing them to identify patterns, make predictions, and perform complex tasks. The quality and quantity of data are critical factors in determining the effectiveness and accuracy of AI models. High-quality data, free from errors and biases, is essential for training AI systems to make reliable decisions. Acquiring and managing large datasets is a significant challenge in the era of big data. Organizations must develop efficient strategies for collecting, storing, and processing data. This often involves leveraging cloud-based solutions and advanced data management tools. Additionally, ensuring data privacy and security is paramount to protect sensitive information and comply with regulations. AI models can be broadly categorized into supervised, unsupervised, and reinforcement learning models. Supervised learning involves training models on labeled datasets, where the correct output is provided for each input. Unsupervised learning, on the other hand, focuses on discovering patterns and relationships within unlabeled data. Reinforcement learning involves training models to make decisions based on rewards and penalties. The availability of massive datasets, often referred to as big data, has significantly accelerated AI advancements. Big data provides AI models with a rich source of information, enabling them to learn more complex patterns and make more accurate predictions. However, processing and analyzing big data requires specialized tools and techniques, such as distributed computing and machine learning algorithms designed to handle large-scale datasets. The increasing reliance on data raises important ethical concerns. Data privacy and security are paramount to protect individuals' personal information. Additionally, biases present in the data can be reflected in the AI models, leading to discriminatory outcomes. It is crucial to develop ethical guidelines and practices to ensure that AI is used responsibly and equitably. The data revolution is far from over. As technology continues to advance, we can expect to see even more innovative applications of AI driven by data. Emerging trends such as generative AI, explainable AI, and AI for social good will shape the future of the field. However, it is essential to address the challenges and ethical implications associated with data-driven AI to ensure that it benefits society in a responsible and sustainable manner.

THE ROLE OF DATA IN AI

Data is the cornerstone of artificial intelligence (AI). The quality and quantity of data directly influence the performance and accuracy of AI models. High-quality data ensures that the model learns from relevant and reliable information, while sufficient quantity of data helps the model generalize to new, unseen examples.

1. Data Quality & Data Quantity

Data quality is a critical factor in the success of AI models. High-quality data ensures that the model learns from accurate and relevant information, leading to more reliable and accurate predictions. Poor data quality can introduce biases, errors, and inconsistencies, hindering the model's performance.

Accuracy:

- Data should be free from errors, such as typos, incorrect values, or inconsistencies. Errors in the data can lead the model to learn incorrect patterns and make inaccurate predictions.
- Data validation techniques can help identify and correct errors in the dataset.

Completeness:

- Missing data can limit the model's ability to learn and make accurate predictions. Missing values can introduce biases and distort the relationships between variables.
- Imputation Techniques: Techniques like mean imputation, median imputation, or mode imputation can be used to fill in missing values.

Relevance:

- Task-Specific Data: The data should be directly relevant to the task the AI model is trying to accomplish. Irrelevant data can introduce noise and confuse the model.

- Feature Selection: Feature selection techniques can help identify the most relevant features and discard irrelevant ones.

Consistency:

- Uniform Format: Data should be consistent in terms of format, units, and encoding. Inconsistent data can make it difficult for the model to learn meaningful patterns.
- Data Cleaning: Data cleaning processes can help ensure consistency by standardizing data formats, correcting errors, and handling missing values.

Data Quantity:

- In addition to data quality, the quantity of data is also crucial for the performance of AI models. A sufficient amount of diverse data is necessary to ensure that the model can learn complex patterns and generalize well to new, unseen data.

Sufficient Samples:

- Learning Complex Patterns: A larger dataset provides the model with more examples to learn from, enabling it to identify intricate patterns and relationships that might be missed with smaller datasets.
- Generalization: A diverse dataset helps the model generalize well to new data, preventing overfitting, which occurs when the model becomes too specialized to the training data and performs poorly on unseen data.

Diversity:

- Bias Prevention: A diverse dataset can help prevent the model from becoming biased towards specific groups or scenarios. Biases can lead to unfair or discriminatory outcomes.

- Real-World Scenarios: A diverse dataset ensures that the model is exposed to a variety of real-world scenarios, improving its ability to handle different situations.

In summary, both data quality and quantity are essential for building effective AI models. A large and diverse dataset that is free from errors and inconsistencies will provide the model with the necessary foundation for learning and making accurate predictions.

2. Data Collection and Acquisition Strategies

Collecting and acquiring high-quality data is a fundamental step in AI development. The choice of data collection strategy depends on the specific application and the availability of data.

Internal Data:

Organizations can often leverage their existing data sources to train AI models. This includes:

- Customer Data: Customer records, purchase history, and feedback can be used to personalize recommendations and improve customer service.
- Sensor Data: Data from sensors, such as IoT devices, can be used for predictive maintenance, anomaly detection, and real-time monitoring.
- Historical Records: Historical data, such as financial records or medical records, can be used to analyze trends and make predictions.

External Data:

- Publicly Available Datasets: There are numerous publicly available datasets that can be used to train AI models. These datasets cover a wide range of domains, including healthcare, finance, and natural sciences.
- Research Repositories: Research institutions and universities often publish datasets related to their research projects.

- Data Marketplaces: Online marketplaces specialize in selling and buying datasets, providing access to a diverse range of data sources.

Data Generation:

- Synthetic Data: In some cases, data can be generated synthetically using simulation techniques or other methods. This can be useful when real-world data is limited or expensive to acquire.
- Data Augmentation: Data augmentation techniques can be used to increase the size and diversity of a dataset by creating new data points from existing ones.

The choice of data collection strategy depends on the specific requirements of the AI application and the available resources. By carefully considering these factors, organizations can obtain the necessary data to train effective AI models.

3. Data Preprocessing and Cleaning Techniques

Data preprocessing and cleaning are essential steps in preparing data for AI model training. These techniques help ensure that the data is in a suitable format and free from errors that could hinder the model's performance.

Data Cleaning:

- This involves detecting and rectifying inaccuracies, inconsistencies, or missing values in the data. Common errors include typos, incorrect data formats, and duplicate entries.
- Techniques like data validation rules and consistency checks can help identify and correct errors.

Data Transformation:

- Scaling data to a specific range (e.g., 0 to 1) can improve the convergence of algorithms and prevent numerical instability.

- Transforming data to have a mean of 0 and a standard deviation of 1 can be useful for algorithms that assume normally distributed data.
- Converting categorical data (e.g., colors, labels) into a numerical format that can be processed by AI models.

Feature Engineering:

- Feature engineering involves creating new features from existing data to improve model performance. This can involve combining features, transforming features, or extracting relevant information.
- Identifying the most relevant features and discarding irrelevant ones can help reduce the dimensionality of the data and improve model efficiency.

Handling Outliers:

- Outliers are data points that significantly deviate from the rest of the data. They can skew the model's learning and reduce its accuracy.
- Outliers can be handled in various ways, such as removing them, replacing them with the mean or median, or transforming the data to reduce their impact.

By performing thorough data preprocessing and cleaning, organizations can ensure that their AI models are trained on high-quality data, leading to improved performance and accuracy. Data-driven AI models rely heavily on data to learn and perform tasks. Different types of learning paradigms are employed, each with its own strengths and weaknesses.

Data-Driven AI Models

Data-driven AI models have emerged as a powerful paradigm in the field of artificial intelligence, revolutionizing industries and transforming the way we interact with technology. These models leverage vast amounts of data to learn complex patterns, make accurate predictions, and perform tasks that were once thought to be exclusively human capabilities. By harnessing the power of data, AI models are enabling breakthroughs in areas such as healthcare, finance, transportation, and customer service. This exploration delves into the core concepts, techniques, and applications of data-driven AI models, providing a comprehensive understanding of their transformative potential.

Supervised Learning:

In supervised learning, models are trained on a dataset where each data point is paired with a corresponding label or target output. The model learns to map inputs to outputs by analysing the patterns and relationships in the labeled data.

- Classification: Predicting categorical outcomes (e.g., spam or not spam, cat or dog).
- Regression: Predicting numerical values (e.g., house prices, stock prices).

Unsupervised Learning:

Unsupervised learning involves training models on data without labeled outputs. The model's goal is to discover underlying patterns, structures, or relationships within the data.

- Clustering: Grouping similar data points together.
- Dimensionality Reduction: Reducing the number of features in a dataset while preserving important information.
- Anomaly Detection: Identifying unusual or abnormal data points.

Reinforcement Learning:

Reinforcement learning involves training models to make decisions in an environment and learn from the consequences of those decisions. The model receives rewards for positive actions and penalties for negative actions, gradually improving its behaviour over time.

- **Agent-Environment Interaction:** The model, or agent, interacts with an environment and receives feedback in the form of rewards or penalties.
- **Learning from Experience:** The agent learns to maximize rewards by exploring different actions and adjusting its behaviour based on the outcomes.

These three learning paradigms are essential building blocks for AI models. The choice of learning paradigm depends on the specific task and the availability of labeled data. In many real-world applications, a combination of supervised, unsupervised, and reinforcement learning techniques can be used to achieve optimal results.

BIG DATA AND AI

Challenges and Opportunities of Big Data

Big data, characterized by its volume, velocity, variety, and veracity, presents both challenges and opportunities for AI.

Challenges:

Big data presents significant challenges in terms of storage, processing, quality, and security.

Storage and Processing:

Storing and processing massive datasets requires scalable infrastructure that can handle the increasing volume and velocity of data. Traditional storage solutions may not be sufficient for large-scale data analytics. Processing big data often demands powerful computational resources, such as high-performance computing clusters or cloud-based platforms. Handling diverse data formats and integrating data from different sources can be complex.

Data Quality:

Large-scale datasets are prone to inconsistencies, errors, and missing values. These issues can hinder the accuracy of AI models and analysis results. Extensive data cleaning and preparation efforts are required to ensure data quality and reliability. Biases in the data can lead to biased AI models, resulting in unfair or discriminatory outcomes.

Privacy and Security:

- Sensitive Data: Many big data applications involve sensitive data, such as personal information, medical records, or financial data. Protecting this data from unauthorized access and breaches is a critical concern.
- Data Privacy Regulations: Adhering to data privacy regulations, such as GDPR and CCPA, is essential to avoid legal and reputational risks.
- Data Security Measures: Implementing robust security measures, including encryption, access controls, and data loss prevention, is crucial to safeguard sensitive data.

These challenges requires careful planning, investment in appropriate technologies, and a strong focus on data quality and security. By effectively managing these challenges, organizations can unlock the full potential of big data and AI.

Opportunities:

- **Improved Decision Making:** Big data can provide valuable insights to support informed decision-making.
- **New Business Models:** Innovative business models can be developed based on data-driven insights.
- **Advancements in AI:** Big data fuels the development of more powerful and accurate AI models.

Big Data Analytics Techniques

To extract value from big data, organizations employ various analytics techniques:

- Distributed computing frameworks that can handle large-scale data processing.

- Databases designed to handle unstructured and semi-structured data.
- Algorithms that can discover patterns and relationships within large datasets.
- Techniques for representing data in a visual format to facilitate understanding and analysis.

Cloud Computing and AI

Cloud computing has emerged as a cornerstone for artificial intelligence (AI) advancements, providing the necessary infrastructure and data storage solutions to fuel AI's rapid development. This synergy between cloud and AI has led to a transformative impact across various industries.

Key Benefits of Cloud Computing for AI

1. Cloud platforms offer unparalleled flexibility in scaling resources to meet the dynamic demands of AI workloads. Whether it's training massive neural networks or handling real-time data processing, cloud infrastructure can effortlessly adjust to varying computational requirements.
2. Numerous AI platforms and tools are now available as cloud services, making AI capabilities accessible to organizations of all sizes. This democratization of AI has lowered the barrier to entry, enabling businesses to leverage AI without significant upfront investments.
3. Cloud-based AI can often be more cost-effective than on-premises solutions, especially for organizations with fluctuating workloads. By paying only for the resources used, businesses can optimize their AI spending and avoid the overhead costs associated with maintaining their own infrastructure.

Challenges and Opportunities in Big Data and AI

While the combination of cloud computing and AI offers immense potential, it also presents certain challenges:

- Handling large volumes of sensitive data in the cloud raises concerns about privacy and security. Organizations must implement robust measures to protect their data from unauthorized access, breaches, and compliance violations.
- Ensuring the quality and consistency of big data is crucial for accurate AI models. Effective data governance practices are essential to maintain data integrity and reliability.
- The rapid evolution of AI requires a skilled workforce with expertise in data science, machine learning, and cloud technologies. Addressing the talent gap is a critical challenge for organizations seeking to harness the power of AI.

To overcome these challenges and capitalize on the opportunities presented by big data and AI, organizations should:

- Build a scalable and secure data infrastructure that can handle large volumes of data efficiently.
- Implement robust data governance practices to ensure data quality, consistency, and compliance.
- Encourage a data-driven mindset within the organization, empowering employees to use data to make informed decisions.
- Provide training and development opportunities to equip employees with the necessary skills to work with AI and big data.
- Partner with AI experts, data scientists, and cloud providers to accelerate AI adoption and leverage their expertise.

These challenges and leveraging the opportunities, organizations can harness the power of AI to drive innovation, improve efficiency, and gain a competitive advantage in today's data-driven world.

ETHICAL CONSIDERATIONS IN DATA-DRIVEN AI

The rapid advancements in artificial intelligence (AI) driven by vast amounts of data have raised significant ethical concerns. As AI systems become increasingly integrated into our lives, it's imperative to address these issues to ensure responsible and equitable development and deployment.

Data Privacy and Security

- Organizations must obtain explicit consent from individuals before collecting and using their personal data. This includes informing them about the purpose of data collection, how it will be used, and their rights to access, modify, or delete their data.
- Implementing robust security measures to protect data from unauthorized access, breaches, and misuse is essential. This involves encryption, access controls, and regular audits.
- Organizations should have clear policies for data retention, ensuring that data is kept only for as long as necessary and then securely deleted.

Bias and Fairness in AI

- AI systems learn from the data they are trained on. If the data contains biases, the AI model will likely perpetuate those biases in its decisions and outputs.
- It's crucial to develop AI systems that are fair and equitable, avoiding discrimination based on factors such as race, gender, age, or other protected characteristics.
- Organizations should actively work to identify and mitigate biases in their data and AI models. This may involve techniques like data augmentation, bias detection, and fair machine learning algorithms.

Responsible AI Development and Deployment

- AI systems should be transparent and explainable, meaning that users should understand how the system works and the reasoning behind its decisions. This can help build trust and accountability.

- Organizations must be accountable for the actions of their AI systems. This includes having clear policies and procedures in place for oversight, monitoring, and addressing potential harms.
- Adopting ethical frameworks and guidelines for AI development can help ensure that AI systems are developed and deployed in a responsible manner. These frameworks may address issues such as human rights, privacy, and fairness.

These ethical considerations, organizations can develop and deploy AI systems that are beneficial to society while minimizing potential harms.

THE FUTURE OF DATA-DRIVEN AI

The field of data-driven AI is evolving rapidly, with emerging trends and technologies promising to reshape our world. This section explores these developments, their potential impacts, and the ethical challenges they present.

Emerging Trends and Technologies

- Models like GPT-4 are capable of generating human-quality text, images, and even code. This technology has the potential to revolutionize content creation, design, and problem-solving.
- Efforts are underway to make AI models more transparent and understandable, enabling users to understand the reasoning behind their decisions. This is crucial for building trust and accountability.
- This approach allows AI models to be trained on decentralized data, preserving privacy while improving accuracy. It has applications in healthcare, finance, and other industries.
- AI is being used to address global challenges like climate change, healthcare, and education. Initiatives are focused on developing AI solutions that benefit society as a whole.

Potential Impacts on Society and Industry

- AI-powered automation will continue to transform industries, leading to job displacement in some areas but creating new opportunities in others.
- AI can deliver highly personalized experiences, from tailored product recommendations to customized healthcare treatments.
- AI can help organizations make better decisions by analyzing vast amounts of data and identifying patterns that humans might miss.
- AI is accelerating scientific research by analyzing complex data sets and identifying new insights.

Ethical Implications and Challenges Ahead

- Ensuring that AI systems are fair and unbiased is a critical challenge. Addressing biases in data and algorithms is essential to prevent discrimination and harmful outcomes.
- The automation of tasks could lead to job losses. It's important to develop strategies to help workers transition to new roles and industries.
- Protecting privacy and security in the age of AI is a complex issue. Ensuring that data is used responsibly and ethically is crucial.
- As AI systems become more autonomous, questions arise about accountability and responsibility. Establishing clear guidelines and regulations is necessary to prevent misuse and unintended consequences.

The future of data-driven AI is filled with both promise and challenges. By addressing ethical concerns and harnessing the potential of AI, we can create a world where AI benefits society as a whole.

CHAPTER FIVE

THE EMERGENCE OF GENERATIVE AI

Generative AI, a subfield of artificial intelligence, has witnessed a meteoric rise in recent years, captivating researchers, developers, and the public alike. This paradigm shift is primarily attributed to the proliferation of massive datasets and the advancement of deep learning architectures, particularly generative adversarial networks (GANs) and transformer models. GANs, introduced in 2014, employ a competitive framework where two neural networks, a generator and a discriminator, work in tandem to produce highly realistic and diverse outputs. Transformer models, renowned for their ability to capture long-range dependencies, have revolutionized natural language processing and are now being applied to other domains such as image and video generation. These powerful techniques have enabled AI systems to generate a wide range of content, including text, images, audio, and even code, often indistinguishable from human-created works. The emergence of generative AI has opened up new possibilities in various fields, from art and design to drug discovery and climate modelling, promising to reshape industries and society as a whole. Fuelled by advancements in deep learning and the availability of massive datasets, generative models have demonstrated remarkable capabilities in generating text, images, audio, and even code. These models, trained on vast amounts of data, learn patterns and structures within the data, enabling them to produce highly realistic and creative outputs. From writing articles and composing music to designing products and generating code, generative AI is revolutionizing various industries and opening up new possibilities.

THE POWER OF GENERATIVE MODELS

Generative models, a class of artificial intelligence algorithms, have emerged as a transformative force in the field of machine learning. These models possess the remarkable ability to learn from vast datasets and generate new, original content that closely resembles the training data. By capturing underlying patterns and structures, generative models can create everything from realistic images and natural-sounding text to complex molecular structures and innovative product designs. This groundbreaking capability has opened up a wide range of applications across various industries, from art and entertainment to science and engineering. As generative models continue to evolve, their potential to revolutionize how we create, innovate, and solve problems is boundless.

TYPES OF GENERATIVE MODELS

Generative models can be broadly classified into three main categories:

1. Variational Autoencoders (VAEs)

VAEs employ a probabilistic approach to learn a latent representation of data. This means they capture the underlying structure and patterns within the data in a compressed form. The process involves two key components:

- Encoder: This neural network maps input data to a latent space, which is a lower-dimensional representation. The encoder essentially extracts the most important features and patterns from the data.
- Decoder: This neural network takes the latent representation as input and attempts to reconstruct the original data. The goal is for the decoder to generate outputs that are as close as possible to the original inputs.

Advantages:

- **Diverse and continuous samples:** VAEs are adept at generating a wide variety of samples that are continuous and smoothly connected. This makes them suitable for tasks like generating images, music, or text where diversity and coherence are important.
- **Dimensionality reduction:** VAEs can be used to reduce the dimensionality of data while preserving its essential features. This can be helpful for visualization, feature extraction, and data compression.
- **Data visualization:** VAEs can be used to visualize high-dimensional data in a lower-dimensional space. This can provide insights into the underlying structure and relationships between different data points.

Disadvantages:

- **Blurry or less realistic outputs:** While VAEs can generate diverse samples, they may sometimes produce outputs that are slightly blurry or less realistic compared to GANs. This is because VAEs introduce a level of randomness into the reconstruction process.
- **Computational complexity:** Training VAEs can be computationally expensive, especially for large datasets. The optimization process can be challenging, and finding the right hyperparameters is crucial for achieving good results.

Case Studies of Variational Autoencoders (VAEs)

Variational Autoencoders (VAEs) are generative models that have found applications in various fields, including image generation, data visualization, and anomaly detection. Here are a few notable case studies:

Image Generation

- **Generating High-Quality Images:** VAEs can be used to generate high-quality images, even for complex and realistic scenes. This has applications in areas such as art, design, and virtual reality.
- **Image Editing:** VAEs can be used to edit images, such as changing the style or content of an image.

Data Visualization

- **Dimensionality Reduction:** VAEs can be used to reduce the dimensionality of high-dimensional data, making it easier to visualize and understand.
- **Anomaly Detection:** VAEs can be used to detect anomalies in data by identifying points that are significantly different from the rest of the data.

Generative Modeling

- **Generating New Data:** VAEs can be used to generate new data points that are similar to the training data. This can be useful for tasks such as data augmentation and synthetic data generation.

Latent Space Exploration

- **Understanding Data Structure:** VAEs can be used to explore the latent space of a dataset, which can provide insights into the underlying structure and relationships between data points.

Drug Discovery

- **Molecular Design:** VAEs can be used to generate new molecular structures with desired properties, such as efficacy and safety.

These are just a few examples of the many applications of VAEs. As the technology continues to evolve, we can expect to see even more innovative and impactful uses in the future.

2. Generative Adversarial Networks (GANs)

GANs are a type of generative model that employ a competitive learning framework. They consist of two neural networks:

- This network is responsible for creating new samples that resemble the real data. It takes random noise as input and generates outputs that are intended to be indistinguishable from real examples.
- This network acts as a critic, evaluating the generated samples and trying to distinguish them from real ones. It is trained to output a probability that a given sample is real.

The generator and discriminator are trained in an adversarial manner. The generator's goal is to produce samples that can fool the discriminator, while the discriminator's goal is to accurately identify fake samples. As the two networks compete, they improve each other's performance over time. The generator learns to produce more realistic samples, while the discriminator becomes better at distinguishing real from fake.

Advantages:

- High-quality and realistic outputs: GANs are renowned for their ability to generate highly realistic and visually appealing outputs. They have been used to create photorealistic images, generate realistic faces, and even produce deepfakes.
- Wide range of applications: GANs have found applications in various fields, including image generation, style transfer, super-resolution, and data augmentation. They can be used to create new content, enhance existing content, and even solve complex problems.

Disadvantages:

- Training challenges: Training GANs can be challenging due to the adversarial nature of the learning process. It requires careful balancing between the generator and discriminator to prevent mode collapse, where the generator produces only a limited variety of samples.

- Mode collapse: Mode collapse occurs when the generator becomes too focused on producing a specific type of sample, limiting the diversity of its outputs. This can make GANs less effective for certain tasks.
- Instability: GANs can be unstable during training, with the generator and discriminator sometimes getting stuck in local minima or experiencing rapid fluctuations in performance. This can make it difficult to achieve consistent results.

Case Studies of Generative Adversarial Networks (GANs)

Generative Adversarial Networks (GANs) have found applications across various domains, demonstrating their versatility and potential. Here are a few notable case studies:

Image Generation

- **Style Transfer:** GANs can be used to transfer the style of one image onto another, creating artistic and visually striking results. For instance, a GAN can transform a photo into a painting in the style of Van Gogh or Monet.
- **Photorealistic Image Generation:** GANs can generate highly realistic images that are indistinguishable from real photographs. This has applications in entertainment, advertising, and virtual reality.

Data Augmentation

- **Expanding Training Datasets:** GANs can generate synthetic data to augment existing training datasets, improving the performance of machine learning models. This is particularly useful when dealing with limited or imbalanced datasets.

Drug Discovery

- **Molecular Design:** GANs can be used to generate novel molecular structures with desired properties, accelerating the drug discovery process.
- **Protein Structure Prediction:** GANs can predict the 3D structure of proteins, which is crucial for understanding their function and developing targeted therapies.

Art and Creativity

- **Generative Art:** GANs can create unique and artistic images, paintings, and music, pushing the boundaries of creative expression.
- **Style Transfer:** GANs can be used to transfer the style of one artwork onto another, creating new and interesting combinations.

Video Generation

- **Video Editing and Manipulation:** GANs can be used to manipulate videos, such as adding or removing objects, changing backgrounds, or altering facial expressions.
- **Video Prediction:** GANs can be used to predict future frames of a video, enabling applications like video compression and anomaly detection.

These are just a few examples of the many applications of GANs. As the technology continues to evolve, we can expect to see even more innovative and impactful uses in the future.

Despite these challenges, GANs remain a powerful and versatile tool for generative modeling. Ongoing research is focused on addressing these limitations and further improving the performance and stability of GANs.

3. Diffusion Models

Diffusion models start with random noise and gradually add information to it through a series of denoising steps. The model learns to reverse this process, generating samples from the original data distribution. Diffusion models are a relatively new class of generative models that have gained significant attention due to their ability to generate high-quality and diverse samples. These models work by introducing noise to the data and then gradually denoising it through a series of steps. By learning to reverse this process, the model effectively learns the underlying data distribution and can generate new samples that are similar to the original data.

One of the key advantages of diffusion models is their ability to generate high-quality and diverse samples. Unlike some other generative models, diffusion models are less prone to mode collapse, which occurs when the model generates samples that are too similar to each other. This makes diffusion models particularly useful for tasks such as image generation and text synthesis.

However, diffusion models can also be computationally expensive to train, especially for large datasets. The iterative process of adding and removing noise can be time-consuming, requiring significant computational resources. Additionally, understanding the theoretical underpinnings of diffusion models can be challenging, making it difficult to optimize their performance.

Despite these challenges, diffusion models have demonstrated impressive results in various applications, including image generation, text synthesis, and drug discovery. As research in this area continues to advance, we can expect to see even more innovative and powerful applications of diffusion models in the future.

Advantages:

- **High-Quality and Diverse Samples:** Diffusion models are known for their ability to generate high-quality and diverse samples. They can produce realistic and detailed outputs, even for complex tasks like image generation and text synthesis.
- **Less Prone to Mode Collapse:** Compared to Generative Adversarial Networks (GANs), diffusion models are less likely

to suffer from mode collapse, a phenomenon where the model generates samples that are too similar to each other. This makes diffusion models more capable of capturing the full range of variations in the underlying data distribution.

Disadvantages:

- **Computational Expense:** Training diffusion models can be computationally expensive, especially for large datasets. The iterative process of adding and removing noise requires significant computational resources.
- **Complexity:** Understanding the theoretical underpinnings of diffusion models can be challenging, making it difficult to optimize their performance and troubleshoot issues.
- **Sample Efficiency:** Diffusion models can be less sample-efficient compared to some other generative models, meaning they may require more training data to achieve good results.

Despite these disadvantages, diffusion models have demonstrated impressive results in various applications and continue to be an active area of research. As researchers develop more efficient and scalable diffusion models, we can expect to see even more impressive results in the future.

Case Studies of Diffusion Models

Diffusion models have emerged as a powerful class of generative models, capable of generating high-quality samples from complex distributions. Here are some notable case studies:

Image Generation

- **High-Resolution Image Synthesis:** Diffusion models can generate high-resolution images with remarkable detail and realism, surpassing the quality of previous generative models.
- **Style Transfer:** Diffusion models can be used to transfer the style of one image onto another, creating artistic and visually striking results.

Text Generation

- **Long-Form Text Generation:** Diffusion models can generate coherent and informative long-form text, such as articles, essays, and scripts.
- **Text-to-Image Synthesis:** Diffusion models can be used to generate images based on text descriptions, enabling creative applications such as storyboarding and concept art.

Audio Generation

- **Music Generation:** Diffusion models can generate high-quality music compositions, including different genres and styles.
- **Speech Synthesis:** Diffusion models can be used to synthesize realistic-sounding speech, enabling applications such as text-to-speech and voice cloning.

Protein Structure Prediction

- **Protein Folding:** Diffusion models can be used to predict the 3D structure of proteins, which is crucial for understanding their function and developing targeted therapies.

Drug Discovery

- **Molecular Design:** Diffusion models can be used to generate novel molecular structures with desired properties, accelerating the drug discovery process.

Diffusion models are a relatively new area of research, but they have already shown great promise in various applications. As the technology continues to evolve, we can expect to see even more impressive results in the future.

APPLICATIONS OF GENERATIVE MODELS:

Generative models have revolutionized various fields by their ability to create new data that resembles existing patterns. Here are some of their key applications:

1. Content Creation

Generative models, a subset of artificial intelligence, have dramatically altered the landscape of content creation. These models are capable of generating new content, such as text, images, audio, and even code, based on patterns learned from existing data. This revolutionary capability has opened up countless opportunities across various domains.

Key Applications of Generative Models:

Natural Language Processing (NLP):

Generative models can produce human-quality text, from articles and blog posts to creative writing and poetry.

They can improve the accuracy and fluency of machine translation systems.

These models enable more natural and engaging conversations with AI-powered agents.

Image and Video Generation:

Generative models can create highly realistic images from simple text descriptions or sketches.

They can be used to generate new video sequences, add special effects, or even create entirely new videos.

Audio Generation:

Music Composition: AI can compose original music pieces in various genres and styles.

Voice Synthesis: Generative models can generate realistic-sounding voices, even for people who are not available to record their own.

Code Generation:

Automated Programming: These models can assist programmers by suggesting code snippets or even writing entire functions.

Bug Detection and Fixing: They can help identify and fix errors in existing code.

Benefits of Generative Models:

- **Increased Efficiency:** Generative models can automate tasks that were previously time-consuming and labor-intensive.
- **Enhanced Creativity:** They can inspire new ideas and help creators explore uncharted creative territories.
- **Improved Accessibility:** Generative models can make content creation more accessible to people with disabilities or limited resources.
- **Personalized Content:** They can tailor content to individual preferences and interests.

Challenges and Considerations:

- **Ethical Implications:** The use of generative models raises ethical concerns, such as the potential for deepfakes and misinformation.
- **Quality Control:** Ensuring the quality and accuracy of generated content remains a challenge.
- **Intellectual Property:** Issues related to copyright and ownership of generated content need to be addressed.

As generative models continue to evolve, their applications will become even more diverse and impactful. By understanding their capabilities and limitations, we can harness their potential to revolutionize the way we create and consume content.

Text Generation

Generative models have significantly impacted the realm of text generation, offering innovative solutions across various domains. Their ability to produce human-quality text has opened up new possibilities for automated writing, creative assistance, and even code generation.

2. Automated Writing:

Routine Content Generation: Generative models can efficiently handle repetitive tasks like product descriptions, news summaries, and social media posts. This frees up human writers to focus on more complex and creative endeavors.

Scalability: These models can generate large volumes of content at a rapid pace, making them ideal for content-driven businesses and organizations.

Creative Writing Assistance:

Generative models can provide writers with fresh perspectives and ideas by suggesting plotlines, characters, or dialogue options. This can help overcome writer's block and spark creativity.

These models can be used to explore unconventional writing styles and genres, pushing the boundaries of creative expression.

Code Generation:

Generative models can generate code snippets or even entire programs based on natural language descriptions. This can significantly speed up the software development process.

By automating routine coding tasks, these models can help reduce the likelihood of human errors and improve code quality.

Key Benefits of Generative Models in Text Generation:

- Efficiency: Generative models can automate time-consuming writing tasks, increasing productivity and efficiency.
- Creativity: They can inspire new ideas and help writers explore uncharted creative territories.
- Accessibility: These models can make writing more accessible to people with disabilities or limited writing skills.
- Personalization: They can tailor content to individual preferences and interests.

Challenges and Considerations:

- Ensuring the quality and accuracy of generated text remains a challenge.
- The use of generative models raises concerns about plagiarism, misinformation, and the potential for harmful content.
- It's important to maintain human oversight to ensure that generated content aligns with ethical standards and is appropriate for its intended audience.

As generative models continue to evolve, their applications in text generation will become even more diverse and impactful. By understanding their capabilities and limitations, we can harness their potential to revolutionize the way we create and consume written content.

3. Image Generation

Generative models have significantly impacted the field of image generation, offering innovative solutions across various domains. Their ability to create realistic and visually appealing images has opened up new possibilities for art and design, gaming, and data augmentation.

Art and Design:

Unique and Creative Images: Generative models can produce images that are truly one-of-a-kind, often surpassing the capabilities of human artists. This has applications in fields like advertising, fashion, and interior design, where visually striking visuals are essential.

Style Transfer: These models can transfer the style of one image onto another, creating interesting and visually appealing compositions.

Gaming:

Dynamic Environments: Generative models can create diverse and ever-changing environments, enhancing the player experience and reducing the workload on game developers.

Procedural Generation: They can generate procedural content, such as characters, objects, or landscapes, ensuring a high degree of variability and replayability.

Data Augmentation:

Synthetic Data Generation: Generative models can create synthetic data, such as images, to augment existing datasets. This is particularly useful when real-world data is limited or biased.

Improved Model Performance: By increasing the diversity and quantity of training data, generative models can help improve the performance of machine learning models.

Key Benefits of Generative Models in Image Generation:

- **Creativity:** Generative models can inspire new creative directions and help artists explore uncharted territories.
- **Efficiency:** They can automate time-consuming image creation tasks, increasing productivity and efficiency.
- **Accessibility:** These models can make image creation more accessible to people with disabilities or limited artistic skills.
- **Personalization:** They can tailor images to individual preferences and interests.

Challenges and Considerations:

- **Quality Control:** Ensuring the quality and realism of generated images remains a challenge.
- **Ethical Implications:** The use of generative models raises concerns about deepfakes and misinformation.
- **Intellectual Property:** Issues related to copyright and ownership of generated images need to be addressed.

As generative models continue to evolve, their applications in image generation will become even more diverse and impactful. By understanding their capabilities and limitations, we can harness their potential to revolutionize the way we create and consume visual content.

4. Audio Generation

Generative models have significantly impacted the field of audio generation, offering innovative solutions across various domains. Their ability to create realistic and diverse audio content has opened up new possibilities for music production, voice synthesis, and sound effects.

Music Production:

- **Creative Inspiration:** Generative models can provide musicians with new ideas and inspiration by composing melodies, harmonies, and rhythms in various styles.

- **Experimental Music:** These models can be used to explore unconventional musical genres and styles, pushing the boundaries of creative expression.
- **Collaboration:** Generative models can collaborate with human musicians, providing a unique and creative partnership.

Voice Synthesis:

Realistic Voices: Generative models can create highly realistic-sounding voices, even for people who are not available to record their own.

Accessibility: This technology can make voice-based services and products more accessible to people with disabilities or limited speaking abilities.

Language Learning: Generative models can be used to create realistic language learning materials.

Sound Effects:

Diverse Sound Library: Generative models can produce a wide range of sound effects, from subtle ambient noises to dramatic explosions.

Customizable Sounds: These models can be trained on specific sound libraries to create custom sound effects tailored to particular needs.

Efficiency: Generative models can automate the creation of sound effects, saving time and resources.

Key Benefits of Generative Models in Audio Generation:

- **Creativity:** Generative models can inspire new creative directions and help musicians and sound designers explore uncharted territories.
- **Efficiency:** They can automate time-consuming audio creation tasks, increasing productivity and efficiency.
- **Accessibility:** These models can make audio creation and consumption more accessible to people with disabilities or limited resources.

- **Personalization:** They can tailor audio content to individual preferences and interests.

Challenges and Considerations:

- **Quality Control:** Ensuring the quality and realism of generated audio remains a challenge.
- **Ethical Implications:** The use of generative models raises concerns about copyright infringement and the potential for deepfakes.
- **Intellectual Property:** Issues related to ownership and licensing of generated audio need to be addressed.

As generative models continue to evolve, their applications in audio generation will become even more diverse and impactful. By understanding their capabilities and limitations, we can harness their potential to revolutionize the way we create and consume music, voice, and sound. Generative models offer a versatile and powerful tool for content creation. By automating routine tasks, providing inspiration, and generating new and unique content, they are transforming the way we create and consume information. As these models continue to evolve, we can expect to see even more innovative and exciting applications in the future.

5. Drug Discovery

Generative models have emerged as a powerful tool in the field of drug discovery, accelerating the process of identifying and developing new therapeutic agents.

Molecular Design

Generative models can design novel molecules with desired properties, such as potency, selectivity, and safety. By exploring vast chemical spaces, these models can identify potential drug candidates that would be difficult or impossible to discover through traditional methods.

Once a promising molecule is identified, generative models can be used to optimize its properties, such as solubility, bioavailability, and metabolic stability. This can improve the drug's effectiveness and reduce side effects.

Protein Structure Prediction

By predicting the 3D structure of proteins, generative models can provide insights into their function and interactions with other molecules. This information is crucial for understanding disease mechanisms and designing targeted therapies.

Generative models can be used to predict the interactions between drugs and proteins, helping to identify potential drug targets and assess the likelihood of drug-induced side effects.

Advantages of Generative Models in Drug Discovery

- **Efficiency:** Generative models can accelerate drug discovery by exploring vast chemical spaces and identifying promising candidates more efficiently than traditional methods.
- **Novelty:** These models can discover novel drug candidates that may not have been considered using traditional approaches.
- **Precision:** By predicting protein structures and drug-protein interactions, generative models can help to design more precise and effective drugs.

In summary, generative models are revolutionizing drug discovery by enabling the rapid and efficient design of new molecules with desired properties. By leveraging these powerful tools, researchers can accelerate the development of new therapies for a variety of diseases.

Data Augmentation

When real-world data is limited or biased, generative models can create synthetic data that resembles the real data distribution. This helps to improve the performance of machine learning models, especially in tasks like image classification and natural language processing.

Generative models can transfer the style of one image onto another, creating unique and artistic compositions. This technique has been used to create art, design patterns, and even video effects.

Artists and designers are exploring new creative possibilities with generative models. By collaborating with these models, they can create unexpected and innovative works of art.

In summary, generative models have a wide range of applications across various fields. Their ability to create new and realistic data has opened up new possibilities for content creation, drug discovery, data augmentation, and art and design. As these models continue to evolve, we can expect to see even more innovative and impactful applications in the future. Generative models can perpetuate biases and stereotypes present in the training data. This can lead to the generation of harmful or offensive content. While generative models can produce impressive results, they may still lack the level of realism and nuance found in real-world data. Developing reliable metrics to evaluate the quality and accuracy of generated content can be challenging. Generative models can be used to create deepfakes, which are highly realistic but fake images, videos, or audio recordings. This can have serious consequences, such as spreading misinformation and undermining trust. The use of generative models raises questions about intellectual property rights. For example, if a model is trained on copyrighted material, who owns the generated content ,As generative models become more advanced, there is a concern that they may displace human workers in certain industries, such as content creation and design.

Training large generative models requires significant computational resources, including powerful hardware and energy. This can be expensive and environmentally costly. As models become more complex, it can be challenging to scale them up to meet increasing demands. Addressing these challenges and limitations is crucial for the responsible and ethical development and deployment of generative models. By being mindful of these issues and taking steps to mitigate them, we can harness the full potential of these powerful tools while minimizing their risks.

CHALLENGES AND LIMITATIONS OF GENERATIVE MODELS

Generative models, while powerful, are not without their challenges and limitations. Understanding these can help us appreciate the ongoing advancements in this field and the areas that still require further research.

Quality Control:

- **Subjectivity of Quality:** The quality of generated content is often subjective and can vary depending on the specific application and the criteria used to assess it.
- **Consistency and Reproducibility:** Ensuring consistent quality and reproducibility can be challenging, especially when dealing with complex models and large datasets.
- **Bias and Fairness:** Generative models can inadvertently perpetuate biases present in the training data, leading to unfair or discriminatory outcomes.

Ethical Implications:

- **Deepfakes and Misinformation:** Generative models can be used to create deepfakes, which are highly realistic but fabricated media that can spread misinformation and harm individuals.
- **Intellectual Property:** Issues related to copyright and ownership of generated content can be complex and contentious.
- **Privacy Concerns:** The use of personal data to train generative models raises privacy concerns and ethical questions.

Computational Resources:

- **Hardware Requirements:** Training and running generative models can be computationally expensive, requiring powerful hardware such as GPUs and TPUs.
- **Energy Consumption:** The energy consumption associated with training and running large-scale generative models can be significant.

- **Scalability:** Scaling generative models to handle large datasets and complex tasks can be challenging, requiring efficient algorithms and architectures.

These challenges and limitations is an ongoing area of research, with advancements in model architectures, training techniques, and hardware accelerating progress. By understanding these challenges, we can develop more robust and ethical generative models that can benefit society in a responsible and sustainable manner.

CHAPTER SIX

GENERATIVE AI IN ART, MUSIC, AND LITERATURE

Generative AI, a subset of artificial intelligence, has emerged as a revolutionary force in the realms of art, music, and literature. By leveraging advanced algorithms and vast datasets, these models can generate original and creative content that rivals human-produced works. This paradigm shift has opened up new possibilities for artistic expression, democratized access to creative tools, and challenged traditional notions of authorship and originality.

Generative AI models have the ability to learn from existing patterns and styles, enabling them to produce unique and diverse outputs. In the realm of art, they can generate stunning visuals, from abstract paintings to realistic portraits. In music, they can compose original pieces in various genres, from classical to pop. And in literature, they can write poems, stories, and even scripts. These models are not merely replicating existing works; they are exploring new creative territories and pushing the boundaries of artistic expression.

A NEW ERA OF ARTISTIC EXPRESSION

Generative AI has ushered in a new era of artistic expression, revolutionizing the way we create, consume, and appreciate art. By leveraging advanced algorithms and vast datasets, these models can generate original and creative content that rivals human-produced works, expanding the boundaries of artistic possibility.

Key aspects of this new era include:

Democratization of Art: Generative AI has made creative tools more accessible to a wider audience, empowering individuals with limited artistic skills or resources to explore their creative potential.

Innovation and Experimentation: These models encourage experimentation and innovation, allowing artists to explore new styles, techniques, and concepts that would be difficult or impossible to achieve through traditional methods.

Challenging Traditional Definitions of Art: Generative AI blurs the lines between human and machine-generated art, challenging traditional definitions of authorship, originality, and creativity.

Collaboration between Humans and Machines: Artists can collaborate with generative AI models, using them as tools to enhance their own creative processes and produce unique and innovative works.

New Forms of Artistic Expression: Generative AI has led to the emergence of new artistic forms and genres, such as algorithmic art, procedural generation, and generative music.

Examples of this new era in action include:

The New Era of Artistic Expression

The advent of generative AI has ushered in a new era of artistic expression, characterized by:

- Unprecedented Creativity: Generative algorithms allow artists to explore new and unconventional artistic territories, creating pieces that would be impossible to produce by hand.
- Infinite Possibilities: The ability of generative AI to produce an infinite variety of outputs opens up endless possibilities for experimentation and exploration.
- Collaboration Between Humans and Machines: Artists are working in partnership with AI models, combining their creative vision with the computational power of machines to produce unique and innovative works.
- Democratization of Art: Generative AI can make art more accessible by enabling individuals with limited artistic skills to

create visually stunning pieces.
- Challenging Traditional Definitions of Art: The use of AI in art challenges traditional definitions and boundaries, expanding the scope of what is considered art.
- Ethical Considerations: As with any new technology, the use of generative AI raises ethical questions, such as the ownership of AI-generated art and the potential for bias in AI algorithms.

Overall, the new era of artistic expression brought about by generative AI is characterized by a fusion of human creativity and machine intelligence, leading to a vast array of innovative and thought-provoking works.

Generative AI has ushered in a new era of artistic expression, characterized by several key trends and innovations:

Innovation and Experimentation:

Pushing Boundaries: Artists are using generative AI to explore new and unconventional artistic territories, challenging traditional norms and expectations.

Unprecedented Creativity: These models can generate ideas and concepts that would be difficult or impossible for humans to conceive, sparking new avenues of creative expression.

Risk-Taking: Generative AI can encourage artists to take risks and experiment with different styles and techniques, leading to groundbreaking and innovative works.

Democratization of Art:

Accessibility: Generative AI tools are becoming increasingly accessible, enabling individuals with limited artistic skills or resources to participate in creative endeavors.

Inclusive Creativity: This democratization of art fosters a more inclusive and diverse creative landscape, empowering a wider range of voices and perspectives.

Breaking Down Barriers: By removing barriers to entry, generative AI can help to break down traditional hierarchies and hierarchies in the art world.

Challenging Traditional Definitions:

- **Blurring Lines:** Generative AI challenges traditional definitions of art, authorship, and originality, prompting us to reconsider what constitutes a creative work.
- **Redefining Creativity:** These models can generate content that is indistinguishable from human-created work, raising questions about the nature of creativity and the role of human intervention.
- **New Perspectives:** By questioning traditional boundaries, generative AI can inspire new ways of thinking about art and its purpose.

Collaboration between Humans and Machines:

- **Synergy:** Artists can collaborate with generative AI models to create unique and innovative works, combining human creativity with machine learning capabilities.
- **Mutual Enhancement:** This collaboration can lead to new perspectives, ideas, and techniques, enhancing the creative process for both humans and machines.
- **Partnership:** Generative AI can serve as a valuable partner for artists, providing inspiration, assistance, and new tools for creative expression.

Emergence of New Forms of Art:

- **Algorithmic Art:** Generative AI has given rise to new artistic genres, such as algorithmic art, which relies on algorithms and computer code to create visual compositions.
- **Procedural Generation:** In fields like gaming and music, generative AI is used to procedurally generate content, creating dynamic and ever-changing experiences.
- **Hybrid Art:** Artists are combining traditional techniques with generative AI to create hybrid works that blend the old and the new.

These trends and innovations are shaping the future of artistic expression, demonstrating the transformative power of generative AI and its potential to redefine what is possible in the realm of creativity.

AI'S ARTISTIC REVOLUTION:

Generative AI, a subset of artificial intelligence, has emerged as a revolutionary force in the realm of art, music, and literature. By leveraging advanced algorithms and vast datasets, these models can generate original and creative content that rivals human-produced works. This paradigm shift has opened up new possibilities for artistic expression, democratized access to creative tools, and challenged traditional notions of authorship and originality.

A New Frontier for Artists

In the realm of art, generative AI models have the ability to learn from existing patterns and styles, enabling them to produce unique and diverse outputs. From abstract paintings to realistic portraits, these models can generate stunning visuals that would be difficult or impossible for humans to create. They can also explore new artistic styles and techniques, pushing the boundaries of creative expression.

Music Composed by Machines

In the world of music, generative AI models can compose original pieces in various genres, from classical to pop. They can generate melodies, harmonies, and rhythms, providing a creative tool for musicians and composers. These models can even collaborate with human artists, creating unique and innovative pieces of music.

AI-Generated Literature

Generative AI has also made significant strides in the field of literature. These models can write poems, stories, and even scripts, demonstrating their ability to understand and generate human language. While they may not yet fully replicate the complexities of human creativity, they can provide inspiration and assistance to writers, helping them to overcome writer's block and explore new ideas.

Challenges and Opportunities

Despite their impressive capabilities, generative AI models are not without their limitations. One of the main challenges is ensuring that the generated content is both original and of high quality. Additionally, there are ethical concerns to consider, such as the potential for AI-generated content to be used for harmful purposes. However, the potential benefits of generative AI are immense. By democratizing access to creative tools, these models can empower individuals to express themselves in new and exciting ways. They can also help to accelerate innovation and creativity, leading to new discoveries and breakthroughs.

As generative AI technology continues to evolve, it is clear that it will play an increasingly important role in the world of art, music, and literature. By embracing this new era of creativity, we can unlock the full potential of human ingenuity and imagination.

THE FUTURE OF CREATIVITY

Generative AI has already demonstrated its potential to revolutionize the creative arts, but its future is even more promising. As technology continues to advance, we can expect to see even more groundbreaking innovations in the realms of art, music, and literature.

Key areas of development include:

- **Enhanced Realism and Quality:** Generative AI models will continue to improve in terms of generating highly realistic and high-quality content, blurring the lines between human-created and AI-generated works.
- **Multimodal Creativity:** These models will become increasingly capable of generating content across multiple modalities, such as text, images, audio, and video, simultaneously. This will open up new possibilities for artistic expression and storytelling.
- **Hyper-Personalization:** Generative AI can be used to create highly personalized content, tailoring it to individual preferences and interests. This can lead to more engaging and meaningful experiences for audiences.

- **Ethical Considerations:** As generative AI becomes more powerful, addressing ethical concerns such as bias, fairness, and the potential for misuse will be crucial.
- **Collaboration between Humans and Machines:** The future of creativity will likely involve a fruitful collaboration between humans and AI, with each contributing their unique strengths and perspectives

Potential societal impacts of generative AI in the creative arts include:

- **Increased Accessibility:** Generative AI can democratize access to creative tools and resources, empowering individuals with limited artistic skills or resources to express themselves.
- **Economic Growth:** The creative industries powered by generative AI can generate significant economic value and create new jobs.
- **Cultural Innovation:** Generative AI can foster innovation and creativity, leading to the emergence of new artistic styles, genres, and forms of expression.
- **Ethical Dilemmas:** However, the rapid development of generative AI also raises ethical concerns, such as the potential for deepfakes, copyright infringement, and the erosion of human creativity.

In conclusion, the future of creativity is intertwined with the development of generative AI. By understanding its potential and addressing its challenges, we can harness the power of this technology to create a more innovative, inclusive, and exciting world of art, music, and literature.

How AI is Redefining Art, Music, and Literature

Generative AI, a subset of artificial intelligence, has emerged as a revolutionary force in the realms of art, music, and literature. By leveraging advanced algorithms and vast datasets, these models can generate original and creative content that rivals human-produced works. This paradigm shift has opened up new possibilities for artistic expression, democratized access to creative tools, and challenged traditional notions of authorship and originality. In the realm of art, generative AI models have the ability to learn from existing patterns and styles, enabling them to produce unique and diverse outputs. From abstract paintings to realistic portraits, these models can generate stunning visuals that would be difficult or impossible for humans to create. They can also explore new artistic styles and techniques, pushing the boundaries of creative expression.

In the world of music, generative AI models can compose original pieces in various genres, from classical to pop. They can generate melodies, harmonies, and rhythms, providing a creative tool for musicians and composers. These models can even collaborate with human artists, creating unique and innovative pieces of music.

Generative AI has also made significant strides in the field of literature. These models can write poems, stories, and even scripts, demonstrating their ability to understand and generate human language. While they may not yet fully replicate the complexities of human creativity, they can provide inspiration and assistance to writers, helping them to overcome writer's block and explore new ideas. Despite their impressive capabilities, generative AI models are not without their limitations. One of the main challenges is ensuring that the generated content is both original and of high quality. Additionally, there are ethical concerns to consider, such as the potential for AI-generated content to be used for harmful purposes. However, the potential benefits of generative AI are immense. By democratizing access to creative tools, these models can empower individuals to express themselves in new and exciting ways. They can also help to accelerate innovation and creativity, leading to new discoveries and breakthroughs. As generative AI technology continues to evolve, it is clear that it will play an increasingly important role in the world of art, music, and literature. By embracing this new era of creativity, we can unlock the full potential of human ingenuity and imagination.

EXPLORING THE INTERSECTION OF AI AND HUMAN CREATIVITY

Generative AI has emerged as a powerful tool capable of generating creative content, challenging traditional notions of authorship and originality. However, the true potential of AI lies in its ability to collaborate with human creators, fostering a symbiotic relationship that can lead to unprecedented levels of creativity and innovation.

Human-AI Collaboration:

Complementary Skills: Humans and AI possess complementary skills. Humans bring intuition, emotion, and cultural understanding, while AI offers computational power, data processing capabilities, and the ability to generate new ideas based on patterns.

Shared Goals: When working together, humans and AI can share a common goal: to create something truly exceptional. This shared vision can drive collaboration and innovation.

Iterative Process: The creative process often involves iteration and refinement. AI can provide rapid feedback and suggestions, allowing humans to experiment and refine their ideas more efficiently.

Examples of Human-AI Collaboration:

- AI can generate musical ideas or patterns that human composers can then refine and incorporate into their own compositions.
- Artists can use AI to generate initial sketches or concepts, which they can then develop and refine using traditional techniques.
- AI can help writers generate ideas, suggest alternative phrasings, or provide feedback on their work.

Benefits of Human-AI Collaboration:

- By combining human intuition and AI's computational power, we can unlock new creative possibilities that would be difficult or impossible to achieve alone.

- AI can automate routine tasks, freeing up human creators to focus on more creative and strategic aspects of their work.
- AI can introduce new perspectives and ideas, challenging traditional ways of thinking and inspiring innovative approaches.

Challenges and Considerations:

- The use of AI in creative endeavours raises ethical concerns, such as issues of authorship, copyright, and the potential for AI to replace human creators.
- It is essential to ensure that humans maintain control over the creative process, preventing AI from becoming a dominant force that undermines human creativity.
- AI models can be biased, reflecting the biases present in the data they are trained on. This can lead to unfair or discriminatory outcomes in creative content.

In conclusion, the intersection of AI and human creativity offers exciting opportunities for innovation and collaboration. By understanding the potential benefits and challenges, we can harness the power of AI to augment human creativity and create truly remarkable works of art, music, and literature.

CHAPTER SEVEN

THE BUSINESS IMPACT: GENERATIVE AI'S ROLE IN INDUSTRY AND COMMERCE

Generative AI, a subset of artificial intelligence, has emerged as a transformative force in the business landscape. By leveraging advanced algorithms and vast datasets, these models can generate original and creative content, revolutionizing industries from marketing and customer service to product design and manufacturing. This paradigm shift has opened up new opportunities for businesses to improve efficiency, reduce costs, and drive innovation.

Generative AI's ability to produce high-quality content at scale has profound implications for businesses across various sectors. In marketing, these models can generate personalized content, improve customer engagement, and drive sales. In customer service, generative AI-powered chatbots can provide 24/7 support, reducing response times and improving customer satisfaction. In product design, these models can assist in prototyping and testing new products, accelerating the development process and reducing costs.

Moreover, generative AI has the potential to disrupt traditional business models by creating new products and services. For example, AI-generated art and music can be sold as digital assets, opening up new revenue streams for artists and creators. As businesses continue to explore the possibilities of generative AI, it is clear that this technology will play a pivotal role in shaping the future of industry and commerce.

MARKETING AND CUSTOMER EXPERIENCE:

Personalized Content Generation

Generative AI has revolutionized the way businesses can interact with their customers by enabling the creation of highly personalized content. These models can analyze vast amounts of data, including customer preferences, demographics, and past behavior, to generate content that is tailored to individual needs and interests. This personalized approach can significantly enhance customer engagement and satisfaction.

Key benefits of personalized content generation include:

- **Increased relevance:** Personalized content is more likely to resonate with customers, as it directly addresses their specific needs and desires.
- **Improved engagement:** When customers receive content that is relevant and interesting to them, they are more likely to engage with it and take action.
- **Enhanced customer satisfaction:** Personalized content can lead to a more positive customer experience, increasing satisfaction and loyalty.

Examples of personalized content generation:

- **Product recommendations:** AI can suggest products or services that are likely to be of interest to individual customers based on their past purchases and browsing history.
- **Personalized marketing campaigns:** Generative AI can create targeted marketing campaigns that are tailored to specific

customer segments or individuals.

- **Personalized news feeds:** AI can curate news articles and other content that is relevant to a customer's interests and preferences.

Improved Customer Engagement

Personalized content generation has a profound impact on customer engagement. When customers receive content that is relevant and interesting to them, they are more likely to pay attention, interact with it, and take action. This increased engagement can lead to a number of benefits for businesses, including:

- **Higher conversion rates:** Customers who are engaged with personalized content are more likely to make purchases or take other desired actions.
- **Increased customer loyalty:** When customers feel that a business understands their needs and preferences, they are more likely to remain loyal to that brand.
- **Improved brand reputation:** Personalized content can help to build a positive brand image and reputation.

Examples of how personalized content can improve customer engagement:

Personalized email marketing: Sending targeted emails based on customer preferences can lead to higher open rates and click-through rates.

Personalized product recommendations: Suggesting products that are relevant to a customer's interests can increase the likelihood of purchases.

Personalized social media content: Sharing content that is tailored to a customer's preferences can make them more likely to follow and engage with a brand on social media.

Chatbots and Virtual Assistants

Generative AI has also played a crucial role in the development of chatbots and virtual assistants. These AI-powered tools can interact with customers in a natural language, providing assistance and support. By leveraging generative AI, chatbots and virtual assistants can generate more human-like responses, improving customer satisfaction and engagement.

Key benefits of using generative AI in chatbots and virtual assistants:

- **Improved conversational ability: Generative AI can enable chatbots to generate more natural and engaging responses.**
- **Increased efficiency:** Chatbots can handle a large volume of customer inquiries, freeing up human agents to focus on more complex tasks.
- **24/7 availability:** Chatbots can provide customer support around the clock, improving customer satisfaction.

Examples of how generative AI is used in chatbots and virtual assistants:

- **Generating natural language responses:** Generative AI can be used to create more human-like responses to customer inquiries.
- **Understanding complex queries:** AI can help chatbots to understand and respond to more complex customer questions.
- **Providing personalized recommendations:** Chatbots can use generative AI to suggest products or services that are relevant to a customer's needs.

PRODUCT DESIGN AND DEVELOPMENT:

Generative AI has revolutionized the product design process by enabling rapid and efficient prototyping. These models can generate a vast number of design options in a short amount of time, allowing designers to explore different possibilities and identify the most promising concepts. This accelerated prototyping can significantly reduce time-to-market and improve product development efficiency.

Key benefits of using generative AI for prototyping:

- **Rapid iteration:** Generative AI can generate numerous design options quickly, allowing designers to iterate on their ideas and explore different possibilities.
- **Reduced design time:** By automating certain design tasks, generative AI can free up designers to focus on more creative and strategic aspects of the product development process.
- **Improved decision-making:** Having access to a wider range of design options can help designers make more informed decisions about product features and functionality.

Examples of how generative AI is used in prototyping:

Generating design variations: Generative AI can create multiple variations of a product design, allowing designers to explore different aesthetics and configurations.

Optimizing product performance: AI can be used to optimize product designs for factors such as functionality, durability, and manufacturability.

Imulating product behavior: Generative AI can simulate how a product will perform in different environments and under various conditions.

Innovative Product Concepts: The Potential for Generative AI to Generate Novel and Creative Product Ideas

Generative AI has the potential to generate novel and creative product ideas that would be difficult or impossible for humans to conceive. By analyzing vast amounts of data and identifying patterns, these models can generate unexpected and innovative concepts that can lead to groundbreaking new products.

Key benefits of using generative AI to generate product ideas:

- **Unconventional concepts:** Generative AI can generate ideas that are outside of traditional thinking, leading to innovative and disruptive products.

- **Diversified product portfolio:** By exploring a wider range of product concepts, businesses can create a more diversified product portfolio.
- **Reduced risk:** Generating a variety of product ideas can help to reduce the risk of product failure by identifying promising concepts early in the development process.

Examples of how generative AI can generate innovative product ideas:

New material combinations: AI can suggest novel combinations of materials that could be used to create new products.

Unexpected product features: Generative AI can identify unexpected product features that could enhance user experience.

Innovative product applications: AI can suggest new and unconventional applications for existing technologies.

Cost Reduction: The Financial Benefits of Using Generative AI in Product Development

Generative AI can help businesses reduce costs in several areas of product development, including:

- **Reduced design time:** By automating certain design tasks, generative AI can reduce the time and resources required for product development.
- **Optimized manufacturing processes:** AI can be used to optimize manufacturing processes, reducing waste and improving efficiency.
- **Reduced product failures:** By identifying potential design flaws early in the development process, generative AI can help to reduce the risk of product failures and costly recalls.

Examples of how generative AI can reduce costs in product development:

Automated design tasks: AI can automate tasks such as generating design variations, optimizing product performance, and simulating product behavior.

Optimized manufacturing processes: AI can be used to identify inefficiencies in manufacturing processes and suggest improvements.

Reduced prototyping costs: By generating multiple design options quickly, generative AI can help to reduce the costs associated with physical prototyping.

Overall, generative AI offers significant financial benefits to businesses by accelerating product development, reducing costs, and improving product quality. By leveraging the power of AI, businesses can gain a competitive advantage in today's fast-paced market.

CONTENT CREATION AND MARKETING:

Generative AI has revolutionized the way businesses create and manage content. By automating various content creation tasks, these models can significantly improve efficiency and productivity.

Key benefits of automated content generation:

- **Increased speed:** AI can generate large volumes of content in a fraction of the time it would take a human.
- **Reduced costs:** Automating content creation can reduce the need for human writers and editors, leading to significant cost savings.
- **Consistency:** AI can ensure that content is consistent in terms of style, tone, and messaging.
- **Scalability:** Generative AI can easily scale to meet the growing content demands of businesses.

Examples of automated content generation:

Blog posts: AI can generate blog posts on a variety of topics, from product reviews to industry news.

Social media posts: AI can create engaging social media content, including captions, hashtags, and images.

Product descriptions: AI can generate product descriptions that are informative and persuasive.

Email marketing: AI can personalize email content based on customer preferences and behavior.

Improved Content Quality: How Generative AI Can Enhance the Quality and Relevance of Content

While automated content generation can be efficient, it is essential to ensure that the content is high-quality and relevant to the target audience. Generative AI can play a crucial role in improving content quality by:

- **Enhancing relevance:** AI can analyze data to understand the preferences and interests of the target audience, ensuring that content is relevant and engaging.
- **Improving readability:** AI can help to improve the readability of content by ensuring that it is clear, concise, and easy to understand.
- **Detecting and correcting errors:** AI can help to identify and correct errors in content, such as grammatical mistakes or factual inaccuracies.

Examples of how generative AI can improve content quality:

Keyword optimization: AI can help to optimize content for search engines by suggesting relevant keywords and phrases.

Sentiment analysis: AI can analyze the sentiment of content to ensure that it is positive and engaging.

Fact-checking: AI can be used to verify the accuracy of information in content.

Social Media Marketing: The Application of Generative AI in Social Media Campaigns

Generative AI has become an essential tool for social media marketing. By automating various tasks and providing valuable insights, AI can help businesses improve their social media campaigns and reach a wider audience.

Key benefits of using generative AI in social media marketing:

- **Personalized content:** AI can generate personalized content for different social media platforms and target audiences.
- **Improved engagement:** By creating engaging and relevant content, AI can help to increase social media engagement.
- **Optimized ad targeting:** AI can help to target social media ads to the most relevant audience, improving ROI.
- **Social media listening:** AI can monitor social media conversations to identify trends and customer sentiment.

Examples of how generative AI is used in social media marketing:

Generating social media captions: AI can generate creative and engaging captions for social media posts.

Optimizing ad targeting: AI can analyze customer data to identify the most effective targeting options for social media ads.

Social media listening: AI can monitor social media conversations to identify customer pain points and feedback.

By leveraging the power of generative AI, businesses can improve their content creation and marketing efforts, leading to increased engagement, higher conversion rates, and stronger brand relationships.

SUPPLY CHAIN MANAGEMENT:

Demand Forecasting: The Use of AI to Predict Future Demand and Optimize Inventory Levels

Generative AI has emerged as a powerful tool for demand forecasting, enabling businesses to accurately predict future demand for their products and services. By analyzing historical data, market trends, and external factors, AI models can provide valuable insights into consumer behavior and help optimize inventory levels.

Key benefits of using AI for demand forecasting:

- **Improved accuracy:** AI algorithms can process large amounts of data and identify complex patterns that are difficult for humans to detect, leading to more accurate demand predictions.

- **Enhanced decision-making:** Accurate demand forecasts can help businesses make better decisions regarding inventory levels, production planning, and resource allocation.
- **Reduced costs:** By optimizing inventory levels, businesses can reduce the costs associated with excess inventory and stockouts.

Examples of how AI is used for demand forecasting:

Time series analysis: AI models can analyze historical sales data to identify trends, seasonality, and other patterns.

Machine learning: Machine learning algorithms can be used to build predictive models that incorporate various factors, such as economic indicators, competitor activity, and marketing campaigns.

Simulation modeling: AI can be used to simulate different scenarios and assess the potential impact of various factors on demand.

Supply Chain Optimization: How Generative AI Can Improve the Efficiency of Supply Chains

Generative AI can play a crucial role in optimizing supply chains by identifying inefficiencies and suggesting improvements. By analyzing data from various sources, such as transportation, warehousing, and production, AI models can identify bottlenecks, optimize routes, and improve overall supply chain performance.

Key benefits of using AI for supply chain optimization:

- **Increased efficiency:** AI can help to streamline supply chain processes, reducing costs and improving delivery times.
- **Enhanced visibility:** AI can provide real-time visibility into supply chain operations, enabling businesses to identify and address issues promptly.
- **Improved risk management:** AI can help to identify and mitigate potential risks, such as disruptions caused by natural disasters or supply chain disruptions.

Examples of how AI is used for supply chain optimization:

Inventory optimization: AI can help to optimize inventory levels by predicting demand and identifying the optimal stock levels for different products.

Transportation optimization: AI can be used to optimize transportation routes, reduce transportation costs, and improve delivery times.

Risk management: AI can help to identify and mitigate supply chain risks, such as disruptions caused by natural disasters or supplier failures.

Risk Management: The Role of AI in Identifying and Mitigating Supply Chain Risks

Supply chains are subject to a variety of risks, including disruptions caused by natural disasters, economic downturns, and geopolitical events. Generative AI can play a crucial role in identifying and mitigating these risks, helping businesses to build more resilient and resilient supply chains.

Key benefits of using AI for risk management:

- **Early warning systems:** AI can help to identify potential risks early on, allowing businesses to take proactive measures to mitigate their impact.
- **Scenario planning:** AI can be used to simulate different scenarios and assess the potential impact of various risks on the supply chain.
- **Risk mitigation strategies:** AI can suggest strategies for mitigating supply chain risks, such as diversifying suppliers or investing in backup facilities.

Examples of how AI is used for risk management:

Predictive analytics: AI can be used to predict potential disruptions, such as natural disasters or economic downturns.

Scenario planning: AI can be used to simulate different scenarios, such as supply chain disruptions or changes in demand.

Risk mitigation strategies: AI can suggest strategies for mitigating supply chain risks, such as diversifying suppliers or investing in backup facilities.

By leveraging the power of generative AI, businesses can improve the efficiency and resilience of their supply chains, reducing costs and mitigating risks.

INDUSTRY-SPECIFIC APPLICATIONS:

Generative AI has the potential to revolutionize the healthcare industry by improving the efficiency and effectiveness of drug discovery, medical imaging, and personalized medicine.

Drug Discovery:

- **Accelerated drug development:** Generative AI can accelerate the drug discovery process by generating novel molecular structures that could potentially be used as therapeutic agents.
- **Improved target identification:** AI can help identify new drug targets by analyzing vast amounts of biological data.
- **Personalized medicine:** Generative AI can be used to develop personalized treatment plans based on a patient's individual genetic makeup and medical history.

Medical Imaging:

- **Enhanced image analysis:** Generative AI can improve the accuracy and efficiency of medical image analysis, such as detecting tumors or abnormalities in X-rays, MRIs, and CT scans.
- **Image generation:** AI can be used to generate synthetic medical images for training and testing machine learning models.
- **Personalized treatment planning:** AI can help to personalize treatment plans based on medical imaging data and patient-specific factors.

Personalized Medicine:

- **Precision medicine:** Generative AI can be used to develop personalized treatment plans based on a patient's individual genetic makeup and medical history.

- **Drug repurposing:** AI can help to identify new uses for existing drugs, potentially accelerating the development of new treatments.
- **Disease prediction:** AI can be used to predict the risk of developing certain diseases, allowing for early intervention and prevention.

Finance: The Application of AI in Financial Services, Such as Fraud Detection and Algorithmic Trading

Generative AI has the potential to transform the financial services industry by improving fraud detection, algorithmic trading, and other areas.

Fraud Detection:

- **Anomaly detection:** AI can be used to detect anomalies in financial transactions that may indicate fraudulent activity.
- **Customer behavior analysis:** AI can analyze customer behavior patterns to identify potential fraudsters.
- **Real-time monitoring:** AI can monitor financial transactions in real-time, allowing for rapid detection and prevention of fraud.

Algorithmic Trading:

- **Automated trading:** AI can be used to automate trading decisions based on market data and algorithms.
- **Risk management:** AI can help to manage risk by identifying potential market trends and predicting future price movements.
- **Personalized investment advice:** AI can be used to provide personalized investment advice based on a customer's individual financial goals and risk tolerance.

Other Applications:

- **Risk assessment:** AI can be used to assess the creditworthiness of individuals and businesses.
- **Regulatory compliance:** AI can help financial institutions comply with complex regulations.
- **Customer service:** AI-powered chatbots can provide personalized customer service and support.

Manufacturing: The Role of Generative AI in Improving Manufacturing Processes and Product Quality

Generative AI can be used to improve manufacturing processes and product quality in a variety of ways.

Process Optimization:

- **Predictive maintenance:** AI can be used to predict equipment failures and schedule maintenance proactively, reducing downtime and improving efficiency.
- **Quality control:** AI can be used to identify defects in products and improve quality control processes.
- **Supply chain optimization:** AI can help to optimize supply chains by improving demand forecasting and inventory management.

Product Design and Development:

- **Accelerated prototyping:** Generative AI can be used to create and test different product designs quickly and efficiently.
- **Product customization:** AI can be used to customize products to meet the specific needs of individual customers.
- **Material selection:** AI can help to select the most appropriate materials for products, based on factors such as cost, performance, and sustainability.

Overall, generative AI has the potential to transform the manufacturing industry by improving efficiency, reducing costs, and enhancing product quality. By leveraging the power of AI, manufacturers can stay competitive in today's rapidly evolving market.

ETHICAL CONSIDERATIONS AND CHALLENGES:

Generative AI, while offering significant benefits, also raises important ethical considerations and challenges. Addressing these issues is crucial to ensure that the development and use of generative AI are responsible and beneficial to society.

Bias and Fairness

- **Bias in Training Data:** Generative AI models are trained on large datasets, and if these datasets contain biases, the models may perpetuate those biases in their output. For example, a language model trained on biased text data may generate biased or discriminatory content.
- **Addressing Bias:** To mitigate bias, it is essential to use diverse and representative datasets and to implement techniques to detect and correct biases in the models.

Intellectual Property

- **Ownership of Generated Content:** Determining who owns the copyright of AI-generated content can be complex. Is it the creator of the AI model, the user who prompted the model, or a combination of both?
- **Legal Implications:** Intellectual property laws may not be fully adapted to the unique challenges posed by AI-generated content, leading to legal uncertainties.
- **Protecting Original Works:** It is crucial to protect the rights of human creators and ensure that AI-generated content does not infringe on existing copyrights.

Job Displacement

- **Automation of Tasks:** Generative AI can automate many tasks traditionally performed by humans, raising concerns about job displacement.

- **New Job Opportunities:** While some jobs may be at risk, generative AI can also create new job opportunities, such as AI engineers, data scientists, and content curators.
- **Adapting to Change:** It is essential to prepare for the workforce changes brought about by generative AI, through education, training, and upskilling programs.

Addressing these ethical considerations and challenges requires a collaborative effort between researchers, developers, policymakers, and society as a whole. By ensuring that generative AI is developed and used responsibly, we can harness its potential to benefit society while mitigating its risks.

These are the generative AI is impacting businesses across different industries. By exploring these areas, you can gain a deeper understanding of the potential benefits and challenges associated with this transformative technology.

CHAPTER EIGHT

THE RISE OF LLMS

Large Language Models (LLMs) have emerged as a groundbreaking technology, revolutionizing the field of natural language processing (NLP). These powerful models are capable of understanding, generating, and translating human language in a way that was previously unimaginable. Built on vast datasets and sophisticated algorithms, LLMs have demonstrated remarkable abilities in tasks ranging from answering questions to writing creative content.

The rise of LLMs has been fueled by advancements in deep learning, particularly transformer architectures. These models are able to capture the complex relationships between words and sentences, enabling them to generate coherent and contextually relevant text. As LLMs continue to evolve, they are poised to have a profound impact on various industries, from customer service and education to research and creative writing.

The development of deep learning architectures, particularly transformer models, has been instrumental in the rise of LLMs. These models are able to capture the complex relationships between words and sentences, enabling them to generate coherent and contextually relevant text. LLMs are trained on massive amounts of text data, allowing them to learn the nuances of language and develop a deep understanding of human communication. The availability of open-source LLMs, such as GPT-3 and BERT, has democratized access to this powerful technology, enabling researchers and developers to experiment and innovate.

In conclusion, the rise of LLMs marks a significant milestone in the development of artificial intelligence. These powerful models have the potential to transform various industries and improve our ability to communicate and understand language. As LLMs continue to evolve, it is essential to address the ethical challenges and ensure that their benefits are harnessed responsibly for the betterment of society.

THE BIRTH OF LLMS LANGUAGE AS DATA

Large Language Models (LLMs) have emerged as a groundbreaking technology, revolutionizing the field of natural language processing (NLP). These powerful models are capable of understanding, generating, and translating human language in a way that was previously unimaginable. The birth of LLMs can be traced back to the convergence of several key factors: advancements in deep learning, the availability of massive datasets, and the increasing recognition of language as a valuable form of data.

Large Language Models (LLMs) have emerged as a groundbreaking technology, revolutionizing the field of natural language processing (NLP). These powerful models are capable of understanding, generating, and translating human language in a way that was previously unimaginable. The birth of LLMs can be traced back to the convergence of several key factors: advancements in deep learning, the availability of massive datasets, and the increasing recognition of language as a valuable form of data.

Advancements in Deep Learning:

Transformer Architecture: The development of the transformer architecture, introduced in the paper "Attention Is All You Need," has been instrumental in the rise of LLMs. This architecture allows models to process sequences of data, such as text, in parallel, making them more efficient and effective for language tasks.

Neural Networks: Deep neural networks, such as recurrent neural networks (RNNs) and long short-term memory (LSTM) networks, have been used to process sequential data, but transformers have proven to be particularly effective for language modeling.

Massive Datasets:

Text Corpora: The availability of large-scale text corpora has been essential for training LLMs. These datasets provide models with the vast amount of data needed to learn the nuances of language and develop a deep understanding of human communication.

Data Quality: The quality of the data used to train LLMs is crucial. Ensuring that datasets are diverse, representative, and free from biases is essential for developing fair and accurate models.

Language as Data:

Language has long been recognized as a vital tool for human communication and expression. However, in recent years, there has been a growing appreciation for language as a valuable resource that can be analyzed and processed using machine learning techniques. This shift in perspective has been instrumental in the development of large language models (LLMs).

Key reasons why language is a valuable resource:

- **Information-rich:** Language is a rich source of information, containing insights into human thoughts, beliefs, and experiences.
- **Diverse Applications:** Language can be used for a wide range of applications, from customer service and education to research and creative writing.
- **Economic Value:** Language can have significant economic value. For example, natural language processing (NLP) technologies are used in various industries, such as customer service, marketing, and finance.

The Role of Data-Driven Approaches:

LLMs have demonstrated the power of data-driven approaches to language understanding and generation. By analyzing vast amounts of text data, these models can learn the patterns, rules, and nuances of language, enabling them to perform tasks such as:

- **Question Answering:** LLMs can provide informative and relevant answers to a wide range of questions.
- **Text Summarization:** LLMs can summarize lengthy texts into concise and informative summaries.
- **Machine Translation:** LLMs can translate text from one language to another with high accuracy.
- **Creative Writing:** LLMs can generate creative content, such as poems, stories, and scripts.

Data-driven approaches to language processing have several advantages over traditional rule-based methods:

- **Flexibility:** Data-driven approaches are more flexible and adaptable to different language tasks.
- **Scalability:** These approaches can handle large amounts of data, making them suitable for real-world applications.
- **Continuous Improvement:** As more data becomes available, data-driven models can continue to improve their performance.

By recognizing language as a valuable resource and leveraging data-driven approaches, researchers and developers have been able to create powerful LLMs that are capable of understanding and generating human language in a way that was previously unimaginable.

Key Developments in LLMs:

- **GPT-3:** OpenAI's Generative Pre-trained Transformer 3 (GPT-3) was a significant milestone in the development of LLMs. This model, trained on a massive dataset of text and code, demonstrated remarkable abilities in a variety of tasks, including generating human-quality text, translating languages, and writing different kinds of creative content.
- **Other Notable Models:** Other notable LLMs include Google's BERT (Bidirectional Encoder Representations from Transformers) and Facebook's RoBERTa (Robustly Optimized

BERT Pre-training Approach). These models have been used for various NLP tasks, such as question answering, text summarization, and sentiment analysis.

The birth of LLMs marks a significant milestone in the field of natural language processing. These powerful models have the potential to revolutionize the way we interact with computers and communicate with each other. As LLMs continue to evolve, we can expect to see even more impressive applications and breakthroughs in the years to come.

CHAPTER NINE

GENERATIVE AI AND LLMS WORKING TOGETHER

Generative AI and Large Language Models (LLMs) have emerged as two of the most transformative technologies in recent years. While they may seem similar at first glance, they serve distinct purposes and can be combined to create even more powerful applications. Generative AI focuses on creating new content, such as images, text, or audio, while LLMs excel at understanding and generating human language. When used together, these technologies can unlock unprecedented possibilities in fields ranging from art and design to customer service and education.

THE POWER OF SYNERGY GENERATIVE AI AND LLMS WORKING TOGETHER

Generative AI and Large Language Models (LLMs) have emerged as two of the most transformative technologies in recent years. While they may seem similar at first glance, they serve distinct purposes and can be combined to create even more powerful applications.

Generative AI:

Creates new content: Generative AI models are capable of generating original content, such as images, text, or audio, based on patterns learned from existing data.

Examples: Image generation, music composition, and text-to-image synthesis.

LLMs:

Understand and generate human language: LLMs are designed to understand and generate human language, making them ideal for tasks such as text summarization, translation, and question answering.

Examples: GPT-3, BERT, and LaMDA.

BERT, LaMDA, and Other Key LLMs

BERT (Bidirectional Encoder Representations from Transformers) and LaMDA (Language Model for Dialogue Applications) are two of the most prominent examples of Large Language Models (LLMs). These models have made significant contributions to the field of natural language processing (NLP) and have been used in a wide range of applications.

BERT

- **Bidirectional Encoder Representations from Transformers:** BERT is a pre-trained language model developed by Google AI. It is based on the transformer architecture, which allows it to process sequences of data, such as text, in parallel.
- **Unsupervised Pre-training:** BERT is pre-trained on a massive amount of text data using a masked language modeling task, where the model is asked to predict masked words in a sentence. This unsupervised pre-training allows BERT to learn the nuances of language and develop a deep understanding of context.
- **Fine-tuning for Specific Tasks:** Once pre-trained, BERT can be fine-tuned for specific NLP tasks, such as question answering, text summarization, and sentiment analysis.

LaMDA

- **Language Model for Dialogue Applications:** LaMDA is a large language model developed by Google AI specifically for dialogue applications. It is designed to generate human-quality text that is informative, comprehensive, and relevant to the topic at hand.

- **Conversational Abilities:** LaMDA is trained on a massive dataset of conversational text, allowing it to engage in natural-sounding conversations with users.
- **Applications:** LaMDA has been used to develop chatbots and virtual assistants that can provide informative and helpful responses to user queries.

Other Notable LLMs:

- **GPT-3:** Developed by OpenAI, GPT-3 is a large language model that has demonstrated impressive capabilities in a variety of tasks, including generating creative content, writing code, and translating languages.
- **T5:** Developed by Google AI, T5 is a text-to-text transfer transformer that can be fine-tuned for a variety of NLP tasks, such as machine translation, question answering, and text summarization.
- **RoBERTa:** Developed by Facebook AI, RoBERTa is a robustly optimized version of BERT that has achieved state-of-the-art results on a variety of NLP benchmarks.

These are just a few examples of the many powerful LLMs that have been developed in recent years. As LLMs continue to evolve, we can expect to see even more impressive applications and breakthroughs in the field of natural language processing.

Synergistic Applications:

When combined, generative AI and LLMs can create powerful applications that leverage the strengths of both technologies. Some examples include:

Personalized Content Generation

Generative AI can create highly personalized content based on individual user preferences, demographics, and past behavior. This can lead to a more engaging and relevant experience for users.

LLMs can ensure that the generated content is coherent, grammatically correct, and relevant to the user's context. This helps to maintain a high level of user satisfaction and engagement.

Creative Writing Assistance

LLMs can provide writers with new ideas and perspectives, helping to overcome writer's block and spark creativity.Generative AI can be used to generate new content, such as plotlines, characters, or dialogue, which can then be refined and incorporated into a creative work.LLMs can provide feedback on written work, suggesting improvements and identifying areas for further development.

Customer Service Chatbots

LLMs enable chatbots to understand and respond to customer inquiries in a natural language, making interactions more human-like and engaging.Generative AI can be used to create personalized responses to customer queries, based on their individual needs and preferences.Chatbots powered by LLMs can efficiently handle routine customer inquiries, freeing up human agents to focus on more complex issues.

Virtual Assistants

LLMs can be used to create virtual assistants that can perform a variety of tasks, such as scheduling appointments, setting reminders, and providing information.Virtual assistants powered by LLMs can be customized to meet the specific needs and preferences of individual users.By automating routine tasks and providing personalized assistance, virtual assistants can improve the overall user experience.

In conclusion, the combination of generative AI and LLMs offers exciting new possibilities for a wide range of applications. By leveraging the strengths of both technologies, businesses and individuals can create innovative and valuable solutions that enhance efficiency, improve customer satisfaction, and drive creativity.

Benefits of combining generative AI and LLMs:

- **Enhanced creativity:** The combination of generative AI and LLMs can lead to more creative and innovative applications.
- **Improved efficiency:** By automating tasks such as content generation and customer service, generative AI and LLMs can help businesses to improve efficiency and reduce costs.
- **Personalized experiences:** These technologies can be used to create highly personalized experiences for users, improving customer satisfaction and loyalty.

In conclusion, the combination of generative AI and LLMs offers exciting new possibilities for a wide range of applications. By leveraging the strengths of both technologies, businesses and individuals can create innovative and valuable solutions.

CHAPTER TEN

THE HUMAN ELEMENT AI AND THE FUTURE OF WORK

The rise of artificial intelligence (AI) has ushered in a new era of technological advancement, transforming industries and reshaping the way we live and work. As AI continues to evolve and become more sophisticated, its impact on the future of work is becoming increasingly apparent. While AI has the potential to automate many tasks and improve efficiency, it is essential to recognize the crucial role that humans will continue to play in the workplace. The future of work will be characterized by a symbiotic relationship between AI and human workers, where each complements the other's strengths and weaknesses. Artificial intelligence (AI) has rapidly evolved, transforming industries and reshaping the way we work. As AI technologies continue to advance, their impact on the future of work becomes increasingly apparent. While AI offers immense potential to automate tasks, streamline processes, and drive innovation, it is essential to recognize the crucial role of the human element in navigating this evolving landscape. The future of work will not be solely determined by AI, but rather by the interplay between human ingenuity, creativity, and the intelligent machines we create. As artificial intelligence (AI) continues to advance, its impact on the workplace is becoming increasingly evident. While

AI offers immense potential to automate tasks, streamline processes, and drive innovation, it is essential to recognize the crucial role of the human element in shaping the future of work.

The future of work is likely to involve a collaboration between humans and AI, with humans focusing on tasks that require creativity, judgment, and empathy, while AI handles routine and repetitive tasks. As the job market evolves, it will be essential for workers to acquire new skills and knowledge to remain competitive. Upskilling and reskilling programs can help individuals adapt to the changing demands of the workplace. It is crucial to consider the ethical implications of AI, such as bias, privacy, and job displacement. Ensuring that AI is developed and used responsibly is essential for a positive future of work. In conclusion, the future of work will be shaped by the interplay between humans and AI. By recognizing the complementary strengths of both, we can harness the potential of AI to create a more efficient, innovative, and equitable workplace.

A PARTNERSHIP FOR THE FUTURE HUMANS AND MACHINES

As artificial intelligence (AI) continues to advance, its impact on the workplace becomes increasingly apparent. While AI offers immense potential to automate tasks, streamline processes, and drive innovation, it is essential to recognize the crucial role of the human element in navigating this evolving landscape. The future of work will not be solely determined by AI, but rather by the interplay between human ingenuity, creativity, and the intelligent machines we create.

The symbiotic relationship between humans and machines has been evolving rapidly, shaping the course of history. From the Industrial Revolution to the digital age, technology has consistently augmented human capabilities and transformed our way of life. As we step into the 21st century, the convergence of artificial intelligence (AI), robotics, and other advanced technologies is poised to redefine this partnership, ushering in a future where humans and machines collaborate seamlessly to address global challenges and create a better world.

The Benefits of Human-Machine Collaboration

Enhanced Efficiency and Productivity: Machines excel at repetitive tasks, data analysis, and complex calculations, freeing humans to focus on creative endeavors, problem-solving, and strategic decision-making. This synergy can significantly boost productivity across various industries, from manufacturing to healthcare.

Improved Decision-Making: AI-powered systems can process vast amounts of data and identify patterns that might be missed by human analysts. By providing valuable insights and recommendations, these systems can support informed decision-making in areas such as finance, healthcare, and climate change.

Augmented Human Capabilities: Prosthetic limbs, exoskeletons, and other assistive technologies can enhance human abilities, enabling individuals with disabilities to lead more independent lives. Moreover, advancements in AI and robotics can help us explore dangerous environments, conduct scientific research, and even perform tasks in space.

Addressing Global Challenges: Human-machine collaboration can play a crucial role in addressing pressing global issues, such as climate change, healthcare, and poverty. AI-powered systems can help optimize resource allocation, develop sustainable solutions, and improve access to essential services.

THE EVOLVING RELATIONSHIP BETWEEN HUMANS AND MACHINES

The symbiotic relationship between humans and machines has been evolving rapidly, shaping the course of history. From the Industrial Revolution to the digital age, technology has consistently augmented human capabilities and transformed our way of life. As we step into the 21st century, the convergence of artificial intelligence (AI), robotics, and other advanced technologies is poised to redefine this partnership, ushering in a future where humans and machines collaborate seamlessly to address global challenges and create a better world.

Key Points:

Historical Context

The journey of human-machine interactions dates back millennia. Early tools, such as the lever, wheel, and plow, marked the first steps toward augmenting human capabilities. These simple tools gradually evolved into more complex machines, such as the watermill and windmill, which harnessed natural forces to perform tasks more efficiently.

The Industrial Revolution, which began in the 18th century, marked a significant turning point in the relationship between humans and machines. The invention of the steam engine and other mechanical devices led to mass production and a shift from agrarian to industrial societies. This period witnessed a dramatic increase in the use of machines to automate tasks, leading to increased productivity and economic growth.

Technological Advancements

Technological advancements have played a crucial role in shaping the evolving relationship between humans and machines. The development of computers in the 20th century revolutionized information processing and communication. Early computers were large, cumbersome machines that required specialized knowledge to operate. However, as technology progressed, computers became smaller, more powerful, and more accessible to the general public.

The emergence of artificial intelligence (AI) in recent decades has further transformed the landscape of human-machine interactions. AI systems can now perform tasks that were once thought to be exclusively human, such as recognizing patterns, making decisions, and even engaging in natural language conversations. This has led to the development of intelligent machines that can learn from experience, adapt to new situations, and collaborate with humans in a variety of ways.

Changing Dynamics

The nature of human-machine interactions has evolved significantly over time, from simple tools to complex systems that can learn and adapt. Initially, machines were primarily used to perform physical tasks, such as manual labor and transportation. However, as technology advanced, machines began to take on more cognitive and intellectual roles, such as data analysis, problem-solving, and decision-making.

Today, the relationship between humans and machines is characterized by a growing level of interdependence and collaboration. AI systems are increasingly being used to augment human capabilities, rather than replace human workers. For example, AI-powered tools can help doctors diagnose diseases more accurately, engineers design more efficient structures, and researchers analyze vast amounts of data to uncover new insights.

Impact on Society

The evolving relationship between humans and machines has had a profound impact on society. Economic changes, cultural shifts, and ethical considerations are just a few of the broader implications of this transformation.

Economic Changes: The rise of automation has led to significant changes in the labor market, with some jobs being replaced by machines while others are created. This has raised concerns about job displacement and economic inequality.

Cultural Shifts: The increasing presence of technology in our daily lives has also had a significant impact on culture. Social media, online communication, and virtual reality are just a few examples of how technology has transformed the way we interact with each other and the world around us.

Ethical Considerations: The development and use of AI raise a number of ethical questions, such as the potential for bias in AI systems, the impact of automation on privacy, and the implications of creating machines that can make autonomous decisions.

As the relationship between humans and machines continues to evolve, it is essential to carefully consider the broader societal implications of these developments and to ensure that technology is used in a responsible and ethical manner. By understanding the historical context and current trends, we can better appreciate the complexities and opportunities presented by the evolving relationship between humans and machines.

THE IMPACT OF AI ON THE WORKPLACE

The advent of artificial intelligence (AI) is reshaping the landscape of work, revolutionizing industries and challenging traditional notions of employment. As AI technologies continue to advance, their integration into the workplace is becoming increasingly inevitable. This chapter will explore the profound impact of AI on the future of work, examining both the opportunities and challenges that lie ahead.

Key Points:

* **Defining AI:** Provide a clear and concise definition of AI, highlighting its key capabilities and applications.
* **AI's Growing Presence:** Discuss the increasing prevalence of AI in various industries, from manufacturing to healthcare and finance.
* **The Future of Work:** Outline the potential implications of AI on the future of employment, including job displacement, job creation, and changes in the nature of work.
* **Challenges and Opportunities:** Introduce the key challenges and opportunities associated with AI in the workplace, such as ethical considerations, skill gaps, and the potential for increased productivity.

The fundamental concepts and potential implications of AI, we can begin to navigate the complex landscape of the future of work.

THE RISE OF AUTOMATION

Automation: A Double-Edged Sword

Automation, the process of replacing human labor with machines, has been a driving force behind economic growth for centuries. However, the advent of AI and robotics is ushering in a new era of automation, with far-reaching implications for the future of work.

While automation can increase efficiency, productivity, and quality, it can also lead to job displacement and economic inequality. As machines become capable of performing tasks that were once the exclusive domain of human workers, there is a growing risk of job loss in certain industries. This can have a significant impact on individuals, families, and communities, particularly in regions that are heavily reliant on industries that are susceptible to automation.

On the other hand, automation can also create new jobs and opportunities. For example, the development and maintenance of automated systems require skilled workers with expertise in areas such as engineering, computer science, and data analysis. Additionally, automation can free up human workers to focus on more complex and creative tasks, which can lead to increased innovation and productivity.

The Future of Jobs in the Age of AI

The future of jobs in the age of AI is a complex and uncertain one. While there is a risk of job displacement, there is also the potential for job creation and new opportunities. The key to navigating this landscape will be to develop strategies that enable workers to adapt to the changing nature of work and to ensure that the benefits of automation are distributed equitably.

Key Points:

- Discuss the potential benefits and drawbacks of automation, including increased efficiency, job displacement, and economic inequality.
- Identify industries that are particularly vulnerable to automation, such as manufacturing, transportation, and customer service.
- Explore the types of jobs that are likely to be created as a result of automation, such as those related to AI development, data analysis, and cybersecurity.
- Discuss the importance of upskilling and reskilling workers to equip them for the jobs of the future.
- Examine the role of governments and businesses in shaping the future of work, including the need for policies that support

workers and promote economic growth.

The potential implications of automation and developing strategies to mitigate its negative effects, we can help ensure a positive future for workers in the age of AI.

THE HUMAN ADVANTAGE

Skills That AI Cannot Replicate

While AI has made significant strides in recent years, there are certain skills that remain uniquely human. These skills are essential for navigating complex situations, solving problems creatively, and building meaningful relationships.

1. **Creativity:** AI can generate creative outputs, but it often relies on patterns and algorithms learned from existing data. Humans, on the other hand, can draw on their experiences, emotions, and imagination to come up with truly original ideas and solutions.
2. **Empathy:** Empathy, the ability to understand and share the feelings of others, is a fundamental human trait that is difficult to replicate in AI. Empathy is essential for building trust, fostering collaboration, and providing compassionate care.
3. **Critical Thinking:** Critical thinking involves the ability to analyze information, evaluate arguments, and make informed judgments. While AI can process vast amounts of data, it often lacks the ability to apply critical thinking skills to complex problems.

The Importance of Creativity, Empathy, and Critical Thinking

These human skills are not only valuable in themselves but also essential for working effectively with AI. As AI systems become more sophisticated, they will increasingly rely on human input to guide their decision-making and ensure that their outputs are ethical and beneficial.

Creativity: Creative thinking is essential for developing new applications for AI and for addressing unforeseen challenges. By combining human creativity with AI's computational power, we can unlock new possibilities and drive innovation.

Empathy: Empathy is crucial for designing AI systems that are user-friendly, inclusive, and respectful of human values. By understanding the needs and perspectives of diverse users, we can create AI that enhances human well-being.

Critical Thinking: Critical thinking is necessary for evaluating the outputs of AI systems and ensuring that they are accurate, reliable, and unbiased. By applying human judgment to AI-generated information, we can avoid errors and make informed decisions.

In conclusion, while AI has the potential to revolutionize the workplace, it is essential to recognize the unique value of human skills. By cultivating creativity, empathy, and critical thinking, we can harness the power of AI while maintaining our humanity.

COLLABORATING WITH AI

The future of work is likely to involve a close collaboration between humans and AI. By working together, humans and machines can leverage their respective strengths to achieve outcomes that would be impossible for either to accomplish alone. This new paradigm of human-AI teams offers exciting possibilities for innovation, efficiency, and problem-solving.

Complementary Skills: Humans and AI possess complementary skills that can be combined to create powerful synergies. Humans excel at tasks that require creativity, empathy, and critical thinking, while AI is well-suited for tasks that involve data analysis, pattern recognition, and automation.

Enhanced Decision-Making: By combining human judgment with AI-generated insights, organizations can make more informed and effective decisions. AI can provide valuable data and analysis, while humans can apply their expertise and experience to interpret the results and make strategic choices.

Increased Productivity: Human-AI teams can significantly boost productivity by automating routine tasks and freeing up human workers to focus on more complex and strategic activities. This can lead to increased efficiency, cost savings, and improved outcomes.

Augmenting Human Capabilities with AI

AI can be used to augment human capabilities in a variety of ways. For example, AI-powered tools can help doctors diagnose diseases more accurately, engineers design more efficient structures, and researchers analyze vast amounts of data to uncover new insights. This can lead to significant advancements in fields such as healthcare, science, and technology.

Key Points:

- **The Benefits of Human-AI Teams:** Discuss the potential benefits of collaboration between humans and AI, including increased efficiency, improved decision-making, and enhanced creativity.
- **Challenges and Considerations:** Examine the challenges and ethical considerations associated with human-AI teams, such as the potential for bias in AI systems and the need for responsible AI development.
- **Success Stories:** Highlight examples of successful human-AI collaborations in various industries, demonstrating the tangible benefits that can be achieved.
- **The Future of Work:** Explore the implications of human-AI teams for the future of work, including the potential for new job opportunities and changes in the nature of employment.

The potential benefits and challenges of human-AI teams, we can prepare for a future where humans and machines work together to achieve extraordinary results.

PREPARING FOR THE FUTURE UPSKILLING AND RESKILLING FOR THE AI ERA

As the workplace continues to evolve, it is essential for individuals to develop the skills necessary to thrive in the age of AI. This requires a commitment to lifelong learning and a willingness to adapt to new technologies and work methods.

Identifying Skill Gaps: Assess the current skills of the workforce and identify the areas where upskilling or reskilling is needed to meet the demands of the AI era.

Developing New Skills: Offer training programs and resources to help workers acquire new skills, such as data analysis, programming, and AI literacy.

Facilitating Career Transitions: Provide support and guidance for workers who may need to transition to new roles or industries as a result of automation or technological advancements.

The Role of Education and Policy in Shaping the Future of Work

Governments, businesses, and educational institutions have a critical role to play in preparing the workforce for the future of work. By investing in education, training, and policy initiatives, they can help ensure that individuals have the skills and opportunities they need to succeed in the AI era.

- **Education Reform:** Invest in education systems that equip students with the skills necessary to thrive in a technology-driven world, including critical thinking, problem-solving, and creativity.
- **Industry Partnerships:** Foster partnerships between businesses and educational institutions to develop relevant training programs and provide students with practical experience.
- **Policy Initiatives:** Implement policies that support lifelong learning, job training, and economic development, such as tax incentives for businesses that invest in employee training and programs to help workers transition to new careers.

By taking a proactive approach to upskilling, reskilling, and education, we can help ensure that the workforce is well-prepared for the challenges and opportunities of the AI era.

A Vision for a Future Where Humans and AI Thrive Together

As AI continues to advance, it is essential to remember that humans will always play a vital role in shaping the future. By understanding the unique value of human skills and working collaboratively with AI, we can create a world where technology serves humanity, rather than the other way around.

- Develop AI systems that are designed to complement human capabilities and enhance our lives, rather than replace us.
- Ensure that AI is developed and used in a responsible and ethical manner, respecting human rights and avoiding biases.
- Make AI accessible to everyone, regardless of their background or socioeconomic status.
- Promote a culture of lifelong learning to equip individuals with the skills they need to thrive in the AI era.
- Foster international cooperation to address the challenges and opportunities presented by AI and ensure that its benefits are shared equitably.

By embracing these principles, we can create a future where humans and AI work together harmoniously to address global challenges, promote innovation, and create a better world for all.

CHAPTER ELEVEN

THE ETHICAL CHALLENGES: BIAS, MISINFORMATION, AND ACCOUNTABILITY

The Ethical Landscape of AI

As artificial intelligence (AI) continues to advance and become increasingly integrated into our daily lives, it is essential to address the ethical challenges that accompany its development and deployment. AI systems, while powerful tools, can also be susceptible to biases, misinformation, and a lack of accountability. These ethical concerns raise important questions about the fairness, transparency, and reliability of AI-driven technologies. Bias in AI systems can arise from various sources, including biased data, biased algorithms, and human biases. When AI systems are trained on biased data, they can perpetuate and amplify existing prejudices, leading to discriminatory outcomes. Additionally, biased algorithms can introduce unintended biases into AI decision-making processes. Moreover, human biases can influence the design and development of AI systems, resulting in unintended consequences. Misinformation and deepfakes pose another significant ethical challenge. As AI becomes more sophisticated, it is increasingly capable of generating realistic but false content, such as deepfakes. This can lead to the spread of misinformation, manipulation, and social unrest. The ability to create and disseminate misleading information can undermine trust in institutions, erode democratic processes, and have serious consequences for individuals and society as a whole.

Accountability is another critical ethical concern in the context of AI. When AI systems make decisions that have a significant impact on people's lives, it is essential to have mechanisms in place to hold those responsible accountable. This includes ensuring that AI developers and users are transparent about the limitations and potential biases of AI systems, and that there are consequences for the misuse of these technologies.

Addressing these ethical challenges requires a multi-faceted approach. It involves developing ethical frameworks for AI development and deployment, ensuring transparency and accountability, and promoting responsible AI use. By addressing these concerns, we can help ensure that AI is a force for good and avoids harmful consequences.

The Importance of Ethical AI Development and Deployment

As AI continues to advance and become integrated into various aspects of our lives, it is crucial to consider the ethical implications of its development and deployment. Ethical AI ensures that these technologies are developed and used in a way that aligns with human values, promotes fairness, and avoids harmful consequences.

Key Points:

- Ethical AI prioritizes the well-being of humans and avoids causing harm. This includes ensuring that AI systems are designed to benefit society and avoid perpetuating biases or discrimination.
- Ethical AI promotes fairness and equity by ensuring that AI systems are not biased against certain groups of people. This requires careful consideration of the data used to train AI models and the potential for unintended consequences.

- Ethical AI requires transparency and accountability to build trust between humans and AI systems. This involves providing clear explanations for AI decisions and ensuring that there is a mechanism for holding developers and users accountable for any harmful consequences.
- Ethical AI protects individual privacy and security by ensuring that data is collected and used responsibly. This includes implementing strong data protection measures and avoiding the misuse of personal information.
- Ethical AI requires human oversight to ensure that AI systems are used appropriately and that their decisions are aligned with human values. This involves establishing clear guidelines for human-AI interactions and ensuring that humans have the ability to intervene and override AI decisions if necessary.

By prioritizing ethical considerations in the development and deployment of AI, we can help ensure that these technologies are used for the benefit of society and avoid negative consequences.

MISINFORMATION AND DEEPFAKES

The Spread of Misinformation

The rapid spread of information through social media and online platforms has made it easier than ever for misinformation to circulate. Misinformation, defined as false or misleading information, can have serious consequences, including undermining trust in institutions, influencing public opinion, and even causing real-world harm.

Social Media and Online Platforms: Social media platforms are particularly susceptible to the spread of misinformation due to their algorithms, which prioritize content that is likely to engage users. This can lead to the rapid amplification of false or misleading information.

Echo Chambers: Online echo chambers, where individuals are exposed only to information that confirms their existing beliefs, can exacerbate the spread of misinformation. This can lead to polarization and a lack of critical thinking.

Bots and Trolls: Automated accounts (bots) and malicious individuals (trolls) can be used to spread misinformation and manipulate public opinion.

The Rise of Deepfakes

Deepfakes, a type of synthetic media that uses AI to manipulate existing content, have become increasingly sophisticated and accessible. Deepfakes can be used to create realistic but false images, videos, and audio recordings, making it difficult to distinguish between real and fake content.

- **Deepfake Technology:** Deepfakes are created using AI algorithms that can manipulate facial expressions, voice patterns, and other features to create highly realistic synthetic content.
- **Potential Harm:** Deepfakes can be used to spread misinformation, manipulate elections, and harm individuals by creating damaging or embarrassing content.

Combating Misinformation and Deepfakes

Addressing the challenges of misinformation and deepfakes requires a multi-faceted approach.

- **Fact-Checking and Verification:** Fact-checking organizations and platforms can play a crucial role in identifying and debunking misinformation.
- **Media Literacy:** Promoting media literacy can help individuals develop the skills to critically evaluate information and recognize the signs of misinformation.
- **Technological Solutions:** AI can be used to detect and mitigate the spread of misinformation and deepfakes. For example, AI-powered tools can be used to identify deepfakes and flag misleading content.
- **Regulation and Governance:** Governments and social media platforms can implement regulations and guidelines to combat the spread of misinformation and deepfakes. This may include

measures such as requiring platforms to label or remove false or misleading content.

By addressing these challenges, we can help ensure that the digital information space is a reliable and trustworthy source of information.

ACCOUNTABILITY AND TRANSPARENCY

The Challenge of Accountability

Holding AI systems and their developers accountable for their actions is a complex challenge. As AI becomes more autonomous, it can be difficult to determine who is ultimately responsible for the decisions and consequences of these systems.

- **Complex Systems:** AI systems are often highly complex and involve multiple stakeholders, making it difficult to assign responsibility for their actions.
- **Unintended Consequences:** AI systems can produce unintended consequences that are difficult to anticipate or prevent. This can make it challenging to assign blame or hold individuals accountable.

Ensuring Transparency in AI Systems

Transparency is essential for building trust in AI systems and ensuring that they are used responsibly. Transparent AI systems provide clear explanations for their decisions and make their underlying algorithms and data accessible to scrutiny.

- **Explainable AI:** Explainable AI refers to the development of AI systems that can provide clear and understandable explanations for their decisions. This can help build trust in AI and ensure that decisions are fair and unbiased.
- **Data Transparency:** Ensuring transparency in the data used to train AI systems is crucial for understanding the potential biases and limitations of these systems.

- **Algorithm Transparency:** Making the algorithms used in AI systems accessible to scrutiny can help identify potential biases and ensure that these systems are used responsibly.

The Role of Regulation and Governance

Regulations and governance frameworks are essential for ensuring that AI is developed and used ethically. These frameworks can provide guidelines for AI development, establish accountability mechanisms, and protect the rights of individuals.

- **AI Regulations:** Governments and international organizations can develop regulations that govern the development and use of AI. These regulations can address issues such as data privacy, bias, and accountability.
- **Governance Frameworks:** Governance frameworks can provide guidelines for the ethical development and use of AI. These frameworks can be developed by industry associations, academic institutions, and civil society organizations.

ETHICAL FRAMEWORKS AND GUIDELINES

Ethical frameworks and guidelines can provide a moral compass for AI development and deployment. These frameworks can help ensure that AI systems are aligned with human values and avoid harmful consequences.

Developing Ethical Frameworks for AI

Ethical frameworks for AI can be developed by considering various factors, such as human rights, fairness, and accountability. These frameworks can provide guidance for AI developers and users on how to make ethical decisions.

- **Human Rights:** Ethical frameworks for AI should be grounded in human rights principles, such as the right to privacy, equality, and non-discrimination.
- **Fairness:** AI systems should be designed to be fair and equitable, avoiding biases against certain groups of people.

- **Accountability:** Ethical frameworks should establish mechanisms for holding AI developers and users accountable for the actions of AI systems.

The Importance of Human Oversight

Human oversight is essential for ensuring that AI systems are used responsibly and ethically. Humans can provide judgment, values, and ethical considerations that AI systems may lack.

- **Human-in-the-Loop:** Human-in-the-loop systems allow humans to review and override AI decisions, ensuring that these decisions are aligned with human values.
- **Ethical Review Boards:** Ethical review boards can provide oversight and guidance for AI development and deployment, ensuring that these systems are used responsibly and ethically.

Ethical AI by Design

Ethical AI by design involves incorporating ethical considerations into the development process from the outset. This can help ensure that AI systems are designed to be fair, transparent, and accountable.

- **Ethical Assessment:** AI developers should conduct ethical assessments to identify potential risks and biases associated with their systems.
- **Ethical Training:** AI developers and users should receive training on ethical AI principles and best practices.
- **Continuous Monitoring:** AI systems should be continuously monitored and evaluated to ensure that they remain ethical and aligned with human values.

By adopting ethical frameworks, ensuring transparency and accountability, and promoting human oversight, we can help ensure that AI is developed and used in a responsible and ethical manner.

CHAPTER TWELVE

THE ETHICAL FRONTIER NAVIGATING THE CHALLENGES AND OPPORTUNITIES

As artificial intelligence (AI) continues to advance at a rapid pace, it is crucial to address the ethical challenges and opportunities that arise from its development and deployment. Ethical considerations are paramount in ensuring that AI is used responsibly and for the benefit of society.

Key Ethical Challenges:

- AI systems can inherit biases present in the data they are trained on, leading to discriminatory outcomes. This can have significant implications for individuals and communities.
- The collection and use of data for AI development and deployment raises concerns about privacy and surveillance. It is essential to protect individuals' personal information and ensure that data is used ethically.
- The automation of tasks through AI can lead to job displacement, affecting individuals and communities. Strategies must be developed to mitigate the negative impacts and create new job opportunities.

- As AI systems become more autonomous, questions arise about their decision-making processes and accountability. Ensuring that AI systems are transparent and accountable is crucial to building trust and preventing harmful consequences.

Ethical Opportunities:

- **Social Good:** AI can be used to address pressing social and environmental challenges, such as healthcare, education, and climate change. Ethical AI development can ensure that these technologies are used for the benefit of society.
- **Innovation:** AI has the potential to drive innovation and economic growth by automating tasks, improving efficiency, and creating new products and services.
- **Human Augmentation:** AI can be used to augment human capabilities, enabling individuals to achieve more and live better lives.
- **Ethical AI Development:** Ethical AI development can foster trust and acceptance of AI technologies, leading to positive societal outcomes.

Navigating the Ethical Frontier:

Addressing the ethical challenges and seizing the opportunities presented by AI requires a multifaceted approach.

Ethical Frameworks

Developing and Implementing Ethical Frameworks for AI Development and Deployment

Ethical frameworks provide a moral compass for AI development and deployment, ensuring that these technologies are used responsibly and aligned with human values. These frameworks can be developed by considering various factors, such as:

- **Human Rights:** AI frameworks should be grounded in human rights principles, ensuring that AI systems respect individual rights and avoid discrimination.

- **Fairness and Equity:** AI should be designed to be fair and equitable, avoiding biases against certain groups of people.
- **Accountability:** Establishing mechanisms for holding AI developers and users accountable for the actions of AI systems is crucial.
- **Transparency:** AI systems should be transparent, providing clear explanations for their decisions and making their underlying algorithms and data accessible to scrutiny.
- **Privacy and Security:** Protecting individual privacy and security is essential when developing and deploying AI. This includes implementing strong data protection measures and avoiding the misuse of personal information.

Once developed, ethical frameworks should be implemented and enforced through various means, such as:

- **Training and Education:** AI developers and users should receive training on ethical AI principles and best practices.
- **Ethical Review Boards:** Establishing ethical review boards can provide oversight and guidance for AI development and deployment.
- **Regulations and Governance:** Implementing regulations and governance frameworks can ensure that AI is developed and used ethically, addressing issues such as data privacy, bias, and accountability.

Education and Awareness

Raising awareness about the ethical implications of AI is crucial for ensuring its responsible use. This can be achieved through:

- **Public Education:** Educating the public about the potential benefits and risks of AI can help foster informed discussions and promote ethical AI development.

- **Educational Programs:** Incorporating ethical AI principles into educational programs can equip individuals with the knowledge and skills to use AI responsibly.
- **Public Discourse:** Encouraging public discourse on ethical AI can help identify and address emerging challenges and opportunities.

Collaboration

Collaboration between researchers, policymakers, industry leaders, and civil society organizations is essential for addressing the complex ethical challenges and seizing the opportunities presented by AI.

- **Multidisciplinary Approach:** A multidisciplinary approach can bring together diverse perspectives and expertise to develop effective solutions.
- **Shared Goals:** Establishing shared goals and objectives can facilitate collaboration and ensure that AI is developed and used for the benefit of society.
- **Knowledge Sharing:** Sharing knowledge and best practices can help advance the field of ethical AI and promote responsible development.

Regulation and Governance

Appropriate regulations and governance frameworks are necessary to ensure that AI is developed and used ethically. These frameworks can provide guidelines for AI development, accountability mechanisms, and safeguards for individuals' rights.

- **International Cooperation:** Developing international standards and guidelines for AI can help ensure consistency and avoid regulatory fragmentation.
- **National Regulations:** Countries can develop their own regulations to address specific ethical concerns and protect their citizens' interests.

- **Self-Regulation:** Industry self-regulation can complement government regulations and provide guidance for AI developers and users.
- **Accountability Mechanisms:** Establishing accountability mechanisms can help ensure that AI developers and users are held responsible for the actions of AI systems.

By implementing these strategies, we can help create a future where AI is developed and used responsibly and for the benefit of society. By navigating the ethical frontier and addressing the challenges and opportunities presented by AI, we can help ensure that these technologies are used for the benefit of society and avoid negative consequences.

CHAPTER THIRTEEN

CONCLUSION

As generative AI and LLMs continue to advance, their impact on society is poised to be profound and far-reaching. These technologies have the potential to revolutionize industries, drive innovation, and create new opportunities. However, they also raise important ethical considerations and challenges that must be addressed. Generative AI and LLMs have the potential to transform various sectors of the economy. In healthcare, they can aid in drug discovery, medical image analysis, and personalized treatment plans. In education, they can provide personalized tutoring and learning experiences. In the creative arts, they can assist with writing, composing music, and generating visual content. These technologies can also be used to develop new products and services, drive economic growth, and improve people's lives.

However, the rise of generative AI and LLMs also raises significant ethical concerns. Bias in AI models can perpetuate existing inequalities and discrimination. Misinformation and deepfakes generated by these technologies can undermine trust and destabilize society. The potential for job displacement and economic disruption is also a major concern.

To ensure that generative AI and LLMs are developed and used responsibly, it is essential to address these ethical challenges. This requires a multi-faceted approach that includes developing ethical frameworks, promoting transparency and accountability, and investing in education and training. By working together, governments, businesses, and individuals can harness the power of generative AI and LLMs for the benefit of society while mitigating the risks. The future of generative AI and LLMs is bright, but it is also uncertain. By understanding the potential benefits and challenges of these technologies, we can work towards a future where AI is used to enhance human capabilities, promote innovation, and create a more equitable and sustainable world. Generative AI and Large Language Models (LLMs) are rapidly emerging as powerful tools with the potential to revolutionize various industries and aspects of our lives. These technologies can generate human-quality text, images, and other creative content, opening up new possibilities for innovation and problem-solving. This refers to a type of AI that can create new content, rather than simply analyzing or categorizing existing data. These are AI models trained on massive amounts of text data, enabling them to generate human-quality text, translate languages, write different kinds of creative content, and answer your questions in an informative way. Generative AI and LLMs can be used to create various types of content, including articles, poems, scripts, and code. These technologies can be used to provide personalized customer support, answering questions and resolving issues efficiently.

Generative AI and LLMs can assist in scientific research by generating new hypotheses, analysing data, and even writing research papers. These technologies can be used to create personalized learning experiences, adapting to the needs of individual students. Generative AI and LLMs can be used to create new forms of entertainment, such as games, music, and movies. Generative AI and LLMs can perpetuate biases present in the data they are trained on. These technologies can be used to generate misleading or harmful content. The ethical implications of generative AI and LLMs must be carefully considered, including issues such as privacy, accountability, and the potential for job displacement. The future of generative AI and LLMs is bright, with the potential to transform various industries and aspects of our lives. However, it is essential to approach their development and deployment with caution and ethical considerations. By addressing the challenges and maximizing the benefits of these technologies, we can create a future where generative AI and LLMs contribute to a more prosperous and innovative world.

www.ingramcontent.com/pod-product-compliance
Lightning Source LLC
Chambersburg PA
CBHW031149130726
47988CB00006B/2604